AMARNA
SUNSET

AMARNA SUNSET

Nefertiti, Tutankhamun, Ay, Horemheb,
and the Egyptian Counter-Reformation

Aidan Dodson

The American University in Cairo Press
Cairo   New York

First published in 2009 by
The American University in Cairo Press
113 Sharia Kasr el Aini, Cairo, Egypt
420 Fifth Avenue, New York, NY 10018
www.aucpress.com

Dar el Kutub No. 4198/09
ISBN 978 977 416 304 3

Dar el Kutub Cataloging-in-Publication Data

Dodson, Aidan
        Amarna Sunset: Nefertiti, Tutankhamun, Ay, Horemheb, and the Egyptian Counter-
    Reformation / Aidan Dodson.—Cairo: The American University in Cairo Press, 2009
        p.   cm.
        ISBN 978 977 416 304 3
        1. Egypt—antiquities—kings and rulers   I. Title
        932

    3 4 5 6 7 8   14 13 12 11

Designed by Andrea El-Akshar
Printed in Egypt

To Dyan: thanks for a wonderful first decade!

CONTENTS

ILLUSTRATIONS

All images are by the author except where otherwise stated.

ix

MAPS

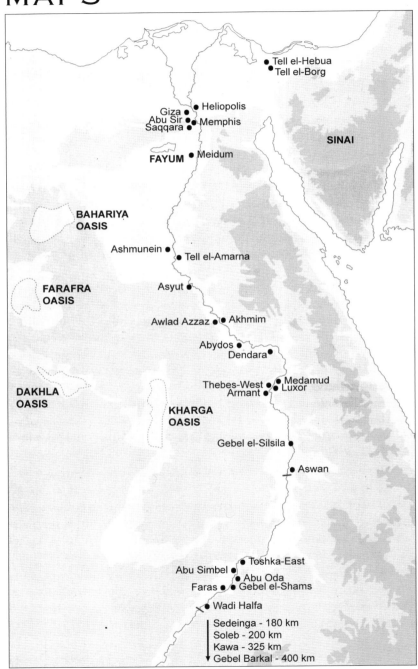

Tell el-Hebua
Tell el-Borg

SINAI

Giza
Abu Sir
Saqqara
Heliopolis
Memphis

FAYUM Meidum

BAHARIYA
OASIS

Ashmunein
Tell el-Amarna

FARAFRA
OASIS

Asyut

Awlad Azzaz Akhmim

Abydos
Dendara

DAKHLA
OASIS

Thebes-West Medamud
Armant Luxor

KHARGA
OASIS

Gebel el-Silsila

Aswan

Toshka-East
Abu Simbel Abu Oda
Faras Gebel el-Shams

Wadi Halfa

Sedeinga - 180 km
Soleb - 200 km
Kawa - 325 km
Gebel Barkal - 400 km

Map 1.
The Nile
Valley

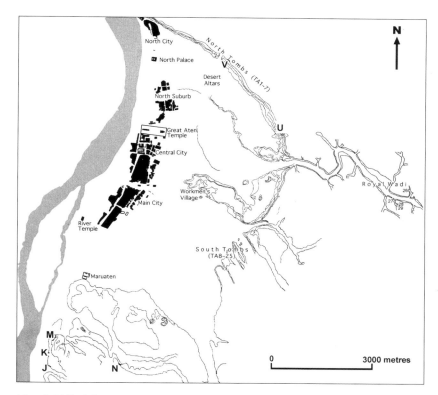

Map 2. Tell el-Amarna

The capital letters indicate the locations of the city's Boundary Stelea that mark out the city limits; a further three stelae were located on the west bank.

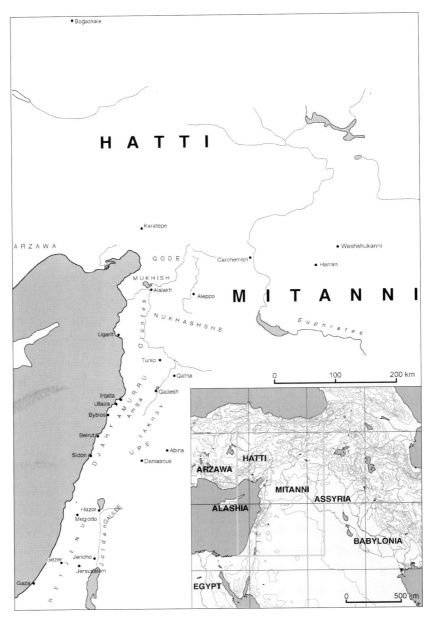

Map 3. The Near East during the fourteenth century BC

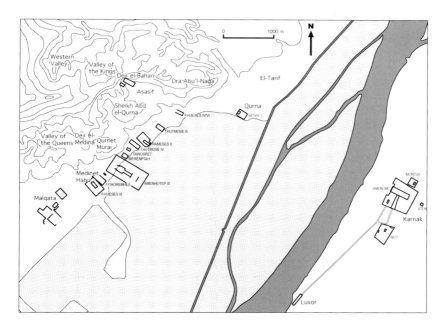

Map 4. Thebes

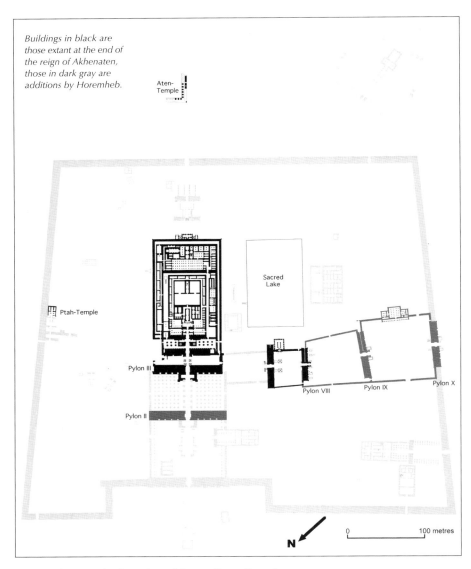

Buildings in black are those extant at the end of the reign of Akhenaten, those in dark gray are additions by Horemheb.

Aten-Temple

Sacred Lake

Ptah-Temple

Pylon III

Pylon II

Pylon VIII

Pylon IX

Pylon X

N

0   100 metres

Map 5. The Temple-Complex of Amun-Re at Karnak

ABBREVIATIONS
AND
CONVENTIONS

Berlin	Ägyptisches Museum und Papyrussamlung, Berlin
BM	British Museum, London
BMA	Brooklyn Museum of Art
Cairo	Egyptian Museum, Cairo
EA	El-Amarna cuneiform letter (followed by number); for translation see Moran 1992 (cf. p. 148 n.5, below)
MFA	Museum of Fine Arts, Boston
MMA	Metropolitan Museum of Art, New York
o	ostracon (followed by current location/number)
OI	Oriental Institute, University of Chicago
p	papyrus (followed by current location/number)
Petrie	Petrie Museum, University College London
RMO	Rijksmuseum van Oudheden, Leiden
SCA	Supreme Council of Antiquities
TA	Tell el-Amarna tomb
TT	Theban Tomb
UPMAA	University of Pennsylvania Museum of Archaeology and Anthropology, Philadelphia
Vienna	Kunsthistorisches Museum, Vienna

Where titles of individuals are capitalized, they are more or less direct translations of the original Egyptian. Persons of the same name are distinguished by roman numerals or letters according to a basic system that has developed within Egyptology since the 1970s—see Dodson and Hilton 2004: 39.

PREFACE

In presenting yet another book on the Amarna Period to the world of Egyptologists, Egyptophiles, and other interested individuals, one feels the degree of trepidation one might otherwise associate with going alone into the zoo tiger-enclosure at feeding time. More so than almost any other era in ancient history, the reigns of Akhenaten and his immediate successors have come to be possessed by a wide variety of individuals, for whom this is something far more than simply a remote period of history. A hint of the widespread usage and abusage of the Amarna Period by people alive in the nineteenth and twentieth centuries AD can be obtained from the lamented Dominic Montserrat's superb *Akhenaten: History, Fantasy and Ancient Egypt* (2000). That book should be compulsory reading for all who consider immersing themselves in the murky waters of Amarna studies.

Part of the problem has been a failure by nonspecialists to appreciate that very little of the Amarna story is indeed fact: much of what we think we "know" is actually (more or less) inspired guesswork based on what Sir Alan Gardiner so rightly called the "rags and tatters" that pass for the raw material of ancient Egyptian history writing. As such, scholarly interpretations can change radically overnight with the appearance of new hard evidence. Indeed, readers familiar with my previous published work on the period will doubtless be surprised that some of the key conclusions of the first half of this book are diametrically opposite to ideas I have vigorously propounded and defended over the past three decades. However, my change of views has been a result of the availability of new data, and it is important to be prepared to reconsider one's position, even if it means repudiating long-held beliefs.

Thus, in spite of a century of further research, many nonspecialists remain convinced that the picture put forward by Arthur Weigall in 1910, and other popular works in the following decades, represent the facts of the Amarna Period. Thus Egyptologists who produce new interpretations can run the risk of being accused of such things as slandering the Founder of Monotheism (note capitalization) or of homophobia when pointing out that it now seems Akhenaten's "gay lover" was actually his (female) wife!

It is partly against this background that the present book has been produced, attempting to put forward an up-to-date presentation of the period from the high point of Akhenaten's reign through to the assumption of power by the Nineteenth Dynasty four to five decades later—in broad terms the last decades of the fourteenth century BC and the first of the thirteenth century. Treatments of this period have generally been overshadowed by the earlier years of Akhenaten, or distorted by a specific focus on Tutankhamun: my aim is therefore to try to produce a balanced view of these decades. Inevitably there are areas where the view put forward is very much my own—in some ways inevitably, given the lack of real consensus among Amarna Period specialists—but I have aimed to indicate areas where alternative interpretations exist, and I have made references to them. In this connection, I must point to the work of Marc Gabolde, whose 1998 book is an essential companion for anyone wrestling with the problems of the Akhenaten/Tutankhamun era. As will become clear, I differ widely from him in many areas, yet without his imagination and dogged research some of the key discoveries that have changed the history of the period—in particular the final proof of the true gender of King Neferneferuaten—might not yet have been made. I must thank him for various stimulating discussions and observations over the years.

I have tried to avoid novelty for the sake of it, and where I put forward or support a view that differs from the received wisdom—rare as that commodity is in Amarna studies—it is because this is either what seems to produce the most coherent scenario, or what sticks most closely to what the bare evidence suggests. On the other hand, the overall picture put forward inevitably depends on assuming the correctness of certain hypotheses—but with the acknowledgment that they are just that and do not claim to be "facts," whatever those might be!

I am sure some readers may object that my characterization of the post-Akhenaten reaction as a "counter-reformation" is anachronistic.

However, I see a number of parallels between the post-Akhenaten situation and that which prevailed in Europe during the late sixteenth and early seventeenth centuries AD. Both involved a reaction to radical religious upheavals (Atenism in Egypt and Protestantism in Europe) by proponents of „orthodoxy," but they combined an attempt to reverse these changes with significant alterations to the nominal *status quo ante* to reflect the new environment. The parallels seems thus not inapposite.

In writing this account, I have attempted to balance readability and accessibility for the more general reader with the demands of scholarship—hence the large swath of endnotes and extensive bibliography. Such a balancing act is difficult, and I am sure Egyptological colleagues would have wished to see more exhaustive analyses of certain points, while the nonspecialists may scratch their heads as to why an apparently esoteric detail is accorded so much space. However, I hope my compromises have not been too heinous. Similarly, translations aim for readability and basic accuracy, rather than cutting-edge grammatical analysis: in all cases, publications of the original texts are accessible via endnotes.

As always in such an enterprise, I have to thank all my various friends and colleagues for their help and stimulus over the years. Although it is always invidious to single out individuals, I must in particular thank Marc Gabolde and Ray Johnson for information, Diane Bergman, Martin Davies, Dyan Hilton, Salima Ikram, Jaromir Malek, David Moyer, Chris Naunton, Bob Partridge, and Cat Warsi for help with images, and Martin, Dyan, Reg Clark, and Sheila Hilton for their most useful comments on the manuscript. Any remaining errors or cases of faulty logic are of course wholly due to me.

INTRODUCTION: SUNRISE

The middle of the fourteenth century BC saw Egypt at the height of her powers. The conquests of the Thutmoside kings of the earlier part of the Eighteenth Dynasty (fig. 1) had created a network of client states stretching some six hundred kilometers up into Syria, while her Nubian possessions stretched a similar distance south of Aswan (maps 1 and 3). From these areas poured tribute and traded goods that made the cosmopolitan court of King Amenhotep III probably the most opulent in Egyptian

Fig. 1. The classic image of Thutmose III as conqueror, on the south face of the west tower of Pylon VII at Karnak.

Fig. 2. The temple at Sedeinga in Nubia, in which Queen Tiye appears in the guise of the goddess Tefnut.

history, the wealth from which financed great new building projects throughout the country. These included major sanctuaries far into Nubia, now a formal viceroyalty stretching beyond the Fourth Cataract. Here in particular the king could be found not simply as a divine ruler, but also as a god capable of being worshiped by his human alter ego.[1] Not only was Amenhotep III a god at Soleb, but his wife, Tiye, was a goddess at nearby Sedeinga (fig. 2).[2]

In his thirtieth regnal year, the king celebrated his first *heb-sed* jubilee; at this his divine essence was further enhanced, and Amenhotep emerging as a solar deity with a markedly changed iconography, in which the aging king is shown as a chubby-cheeked child with almond-shaped eyes (fig. 3).[3] This emphasis on solar cults is evident from earlier in the dynasty, in particular with an increasing promotion of the god Aten, a manifestation of the long-established Re-Horakhty, first seen as an independent deity under Thutmose IV. During Amenhotep III's reign, a state barge was named "Radiance of the Aten" by Year 11, as was the West Theban palace at Malqata prior to the king's first jubilee. However, the traditional gods continued to enjoy full royal patronage, not only through the foundation and extension of temples, but also through the appointment of the crown prince, Thutmose (B), first as *sem*-Priest of Ptah at Memphis, and then as high priest there (fig. 4).[4]

Fig. 3. Amenhotep III in the art style adopted after his first jubilee (Luxor Museum).

Fig. 4. Crown Prince Thutmose B, as depicted in the shrine of Apis I at Saqqara (Munich Gl.93, on loan to Berlin).

Fig. 5. Relief, reused in the core of Pylon X at Karnak, of the Aten and Amenhotep IV in conventional style (Berlin 2072).

    The appointment of Thutmose to this pontificate was a feature of a gradual increase in the profile of royal princes during the first part of the New Kingdom.[5] During the Fourth Dynasty, sons and grandsons of the king had held some of the highest offices of the state,[6] but in subsequent dynasties they had become all but invisible in the surviving record.[7] Then, during the Eighteenth Dynasty reign of Thutmose I, his eldest son Amenmose appears with a high military title,[8] followed by Thutmose III's heir Amenemhat B,[9] who received the office of Overseer of Cattle in his father's Year 24.[10] A King's Son Amenhotep (B/C) became *sem*-Priest of Ptah under

Fig. 6. Stela showing
the Aten in conventional
style, but with cartouches
(Edinburgh A.1956.347).

either Thutmose III or Amenhotep II,[11] and under Thutmose IV a King's Son (Ahmose B) functioned as high priest at Heliopolis.[12] Both these appointments clearly form part of a pattern of appointing royal princes to senior priestly roles in national cults—although, interestingly, apparently not that of Amun-Re at Karnak. This approach was later also adopted by the Ramesside kings of the Nineteenth and Twentieth Dynasties.[13]

This reappearance of royal princes is paralleled to a somewhat different degree among the royal daughters, who are prominent in relief commemorating the jubilees celebrated by Amenhotep III from Year 30 onward,[14] as well as accompanying their parents on statuary.[15] The royal sons are not, however, found in such contexts,[16] and thus a second son, Amenhotep E, is known only from a seal impression from Amenhotep III's palace complex at Malqata.[17] It was this son who succeeded to the throne as Amenhotep IV, Thutmose having died prematurely, possibly around Year 30, as is suggested by a cryptic contemporary graffito that could be read as recording the formal nomination of a (new) heir in that year.[18]

The debate as to whether Amenhotep IV succeeded Amenhotep III after a period of co-rule or only on the latter's death has generated a vast literature, with the battle between the two camps ebbing and flowing over the decades on the basis of the equivocal nature of the evidence.[19] However, the weight of evidence currently seems to lie in favor of the view that Amenhotep IV's accession only followed his father's demise,[20] and that juxtapositions of the two kings on monuments[21] or images of Amenhotep III in later artistic styles[22] should be taken as memorials.

That these should exceed in number those known to have been produced in earlier times for deceased pharaohs may be another manifestation of the enhanced concept of a "royal family," which now becomes even more significant in the new reign. This goes hand in hand with the most significant aspect of Amenhotep IV's regime, which is the rapid promotion of the Aten from a merely favored deity into a supreme—if not yet sole—god during the first few years of the reign.

The earliest monuments to the Aten employ traditional forms: an anthropomorphic image of the god, with his long didactic name written like the epithets of other gods without any special enclosure (fig. 5). That name rapidly gains a pair of enclosing cartouches (fig. 6)[23] before the depiction of the god switches to the abstract form of a sun disk with descending rays (fig. 7).[24]

This switch in the iconography of the god was rapidly followed by a dramatic change in the way the king—and by extension the rest of humanity—

Fig. 7. A Karnak relief showing Amenhotep IV (with his nomen surcharged as Akhenaten) in a proto-Amarna style, worshiping one of the earliest known abstract depictions of the Aten (Louvre E13482*ter*).

Fig. 8. Stela of the Amarna royal family in the classic Amarna style. From Amarna (Berlin 14145).

was depicted (fig. 8).[25] Some of the earliest examples of this new style are to be found in the temple of the Aten that Amenhotep IV—soon to be Akhenaten—built in the northern sector of the Karnak precinct (map 5).[26] Some of the depictions in this sanctuary indicate that early in the king's reign a *heb-sed* jubilee celebration was held, not (as one would normally expect) as that of the king, but apparently of the Aten.[27] This would reflect the status of the Aten as a heavenly king, already indicated by his adoption of royal cartouches around the same time.

In spite of this major building at Karnak, by Year 4 a decision had been taken to found a city to act both as the home of the Aten cult and the new principal royal residence, at a site now known as Tell el-Amarna, its limits set by a series of boundary stelae dated to Years 4 and 5 (map 2).[28] These marked out a slice across the Nile valley, comprising a fertile area on the west bank, and a more arid district on the east bank in which the urban area was constructed.[29] It was named Akhet-Aten—the Horizon of Aten.

On these boundary markers, Akhenaten—as he now was—is joined by his wife Nefertiti, and elder daughters Meryetaten and Meketaten. Nefertiti's name is expanded to Neferneferuaten-Nefertiti soon after her husband's change of nomen in Year 5 (appendix 2). The royal family is writ large across

8   INTRODUCTION

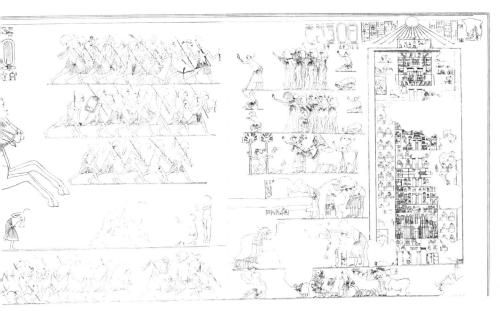

Fig. 9. The royal family processes in chariots to the Aten temple, escorted by running soldiers, in the tomb of Meryre i (TA4).

the broad swath of monuments produced during the reign, not only in ritual scenes in the temples of Amarna and Thebes, but also in the private tomb-chapels. Here, the customary motifs of daily life are replaced by large tableaux of the royal family going about their business, the tomb owner being relegated to a subsidiary figure. In the new Amarna milieu, the royal family stood as the sole intermediary between humankind and the deity, as was shown neatly in the chapels of private houses where the object of devotion was not the physical sun above, but a stela showing the royal family adoring the sun on their behalf.[30]

Vast open-air temples in which massive quantities of food and drink were placed on offering tables for the benefit of the sun,[31] together with the official palace of the king and various government offices, were an important component of the central city at Amarna. North and south of this spread a series of residential suburbs and, at the northern extremity of the city, the so-called North City incorporated the royal family's regular residence. This was connected to the central city by the royal road, along which the king's chariot and entourage undertook a ceremonial daily progress, a motif frequently employed in the decoration of the private tomb-chapels (fig. 9).

These sepulchers were located in the cliffs in the northeastern sector of the city, and in low hills in the southeast quadrant. As already noted, they differed fundamentally in decoration from those at Thebes; architecturally they were rather more a mix of old and new.[32] An area to mirror the Valley of the Kings was also established in the eastern hills, where the king, his family, and his successors were to be buried.[33]

Following the formal establishment of Akhet-Aten in Years 4/5, no specific dates can be attributed to events during the first half-dozen years of the city's existence, which presumably saw its progressive construction, occupation, and expansion. However, at some point during this time the cartouche names of the Aten underwent a fundamental change: rather than being "Living Re-Horakhty, who rejoices in the horizon in his name Shu-Re who is in Aten," the god becomes "Living Re, ruler of the horizon, who rejoices in his name of Re the father who has returned as Aten." The key change here is that the old air god Shu is dropped from the Aten's nature, as is the explicit link with Re-Horakhty, seen in the Aten's original anthropomorphic manifestation.

The change, which on occasion was accompanied by a changing of early cartouches to the later ones,[34] seems to have happened between Year 8, when the early form was still being used in that year's colophon on boundary stelae A and B,[35] and Year 12 when the later form appears in dated tableaux in two Amarna tombs.[36] It has generally been assumed that the change actually took place in Year 9, but this is based on old assumptions as to the relative ages of Akhenaten's daughters, which are not necessarily valid.[37]

In any case, it seems clear that much of the construction of the city of Akhet-Aten was well under way by the time the change took place.[38] Thus by Year 12 it is likely that the city was to all intents and purposes complete, and a suitable backdrop for an event that seemingly marked the high watermark of Akhenaten's reign.

1 THE NOONDAY SUN

"**Y**ear 12, II *prt*, day 8: [the king and queen] appeared on the great carrying-chair of gold to receive the tribute of Kharu [Syria-Palestine: map 2] and Kush [Nubia], the West and the East. All countries collected together at one time, and the lands in the midst of the sea, bringing offerings to the king upon the great throne of Akhet-Aten for receiving the goods of every land, granting to them the breath of life." This text appears as a caption to a tableau occupying the whole of the west wall of the first hall of the tomb-chapel of Huya, steward of Queen Tiye (TA1: fig. 10, top). A very similar, but more summary, text is to be found in another large tableau on the east wall of the first room of the next-door tomb-chapel of the royal scribe Meryre ii (TA2: fig. 10, bottom).

The two tableaux are different from one another, apparently showing respectively the royal couple's approach to the location of the festivities in their carrying-chair, and their oversight of the *durbar* itself from a kiosk, the latter being the more detailed representation. However, they both feature extensive depictions of raw materials and manufactured goods, and of man-acled individuals—Syrian and Nubian in appearance—brought by several distinct delegations, recognizable iconographically as including Nubians,[1] Syrians, Hittites, and possibly Amorites.

The *durbar*'s great international gathering was clearly a particularly significant event in Akhenaten's career, with much of the known world bringing gifts to the king. However, the import of the event itself remains obscure. The precise date given in both label-texts[2] shows it to be a record of a specific event, and not a generic icon—but why was it occurring then?

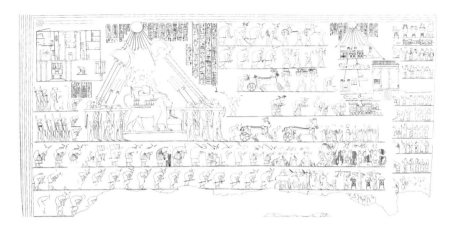

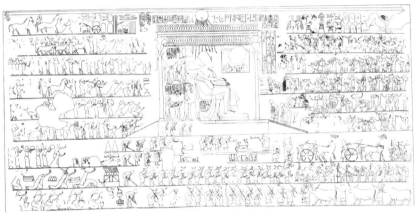

Fig. 10. *Durbar* scenes in the tomb-chapels of Huya (TA1, top) and Meryre ii (TA2, bottom).

Those who have espoused the idea of a long coregency between Akhenaten and Amenhotep III have argued that it might mark part of the celebration of the transition to Akhenaten's sole rule. However, if there was indeed no coregency of this kind,[3] one is left looking for other explanations.

It may be that such events took place periodically during the Eighteenth Dynasty, and it is only the exceptional nature of Amarna tomb-iconography that means this particular one is depicted and dated: similar events may indeed have taken place under earlier kings, but would not form part of the pre-Amarna tomb-chapel repertoire. The breadth of the attendance and the overall context would suggest it was not simply the outcome of successful military action, although at some time during Years 10–12 Akhenaten's armies had scored a victory somewhere in the vicinity of the Wadi el-Allaqi, about three hundred kilometers east of Wadi Halfa.[4] Alternatively, might one see in it an international celebration of the completion of Akhenaten's great project—given that work had by now been going on for some seven years—the king showing off to the world his model capital city, and the glory of the Aten?

The *durbar* scenes are also interesting from the point of view of the royal family, as showing its public extent on that day in Year 12 (for a tentative royal genealogical chart of the period, see appendix 3). In most of the tomb-chapels at Amarna, a maximum of four daughters are shown—Meryetaten, Meketaten, Ankhesenpaaten, and Neferneferuaten-tasherit. The gradual addition to their number has on occasion been used to relatively date individual tomb-chapels, but the vagaries of laying out the decoration of a wall make this problematic. This is shown clearly when comparing the scenes in TA1 and TA2: in the former, only two daughters are unequivocally shown and named—Meryetaten and Meketaten—with perhaps one or two others shown on a smaller scale, but not named.[5] Indeed, throughout TA1 only two girls seem ever to be shown in any one scene, although four appear cumulatively around the tomb.[6]

On the other hand, in TA2 we find no fewer than six daughters, now including two (Neferneferure and Setepenre) who are not found in any other Amarna tomb-chapels.They thus presumably only became old enough to be acknowledged—i.e., lived long enough to have some chance of longer-term survival—just before Year 12. That this was particularly true for Setepenre is suggested by the fact that while Neferneferure is seen in a reward scene on the south wall of TA2, Setepenre is not. One might therefore suggest that Neferneferure was born around Year 9/10,[7] and Setepenre in Year 10/11 (fig. 11).[8]

While we thus have six daughters of Akhenaten and Nefertiti alive in Year 12, it is quite possible that other children may have been born during their years of marriage, which presumably went back to the earliest years of the reign of Amenhotep IV, as he then was.[9] Given the level of premodern infant mortality, it is likely that some could have died without featuring on the monuments. It is also not unlikely that boys were born as well as girls, but any who might have survived infancy would also generally have missed monumental commemoration by the decorum that had apparently excluded princes from royal family tableaux for generations. Looking back through Egyptian history, royal sons are conspicuous by their absence

Fig. 11. The growth of the royal family as recorded in the tomb of Meryre ii: on the left, in the reward scene on the south wall, from top right: Ankhesenpaaten, Neferneferuaten-tasherit, Neferneferure, Meryetaten, and Meketaten; on the right, in the *durbar* scene on the east wall: [Meryetaten], Meketaten, Ankhesenpaaten, Neferneferuaten-tasherit, Neferneferure, and Setepenre.

Fig. 12. A pair of blocks at Ashmunein bearing the names of Prince Tutankhuaten on the right, and a princess (whose name is damaged) on the left. They may have come from a semi-symmetrical scene of Akhenaten and Nefertiti worshiping the Aten, with their children divided between them (Supreme Council of Antiquities storeroom at Ashmunein).

from the monuments, apart from the short period during the Fourth Dynasty when many held key offices of state:[10] indeed, during the Middle Kingdom only two princes are known. Our first real glimpse into the world of the kings' sons is only gained when the practice began of assigning princes to nobles for their education. Then, the subsequent desire of these worthies to commemorate this signal honour on their own monuments gives us the names of New Kingdom princes who would otherwise be unknown. In addition, certain sons were given formal posts in the priesthoods, and thus can appear on monuments in that guise—for example, Prince Thutmose B, elder son of Amenhotep III, who appears in the funerary chapel of the contemporary Apis bull[11] by virtue of his office as high priest of Ptah. However, in the very same reign, Amenhotep III is accompanied only by his wife and daughters where the "royal family" icon is being used, whether in two or three dimensions.[12]

    Thus the absence of male children depicted among Akhenaten and Nefertiti's brood in the Amarna tombs should by no means be taken as indicating they had no such offspring. That there was a male royal child at Amarna is shown by a block found at Ashmunein[13] (brought across from Amarna as building stone under Rameses II) mentioning a "King's Son of [his] body, his beloved Tutankhuaten" (fig. 12). The latter seems to have been shown facing a princess whose name, on the adjacent block, is unfortunately now lost, apart from the "-Aten" element.[14] Coming from an Amarna temple,

Fig. 13. Relief of Kiya, with head altered and inscription recut to serve as a representation of Meryetaten. From Ashmunein (Copenhagen Ny Carlsberg ÆIN 1775).

the block's status as a strong piece of evidence for Akhenaten's paternity of Tutankhuaten has now been fairly generally admitted by scholars.[15]

On the other hand, the identity of the child's mother has been much debated. Nefertiti has generally been dismissed out of hand, essentially on the basis of the prince's absence from the family groups at Amarna. With her out of the way, other than appealing to the existence of some unknown "secondary wife or concubine,"[16] the most often cited candidate for Tutankhuaten's mother has been the Greatly Beloved Wife (*ḥmt-mrrty-ˁȝt*) Kiya.[17]

This lady has always been something of a mystery. Her title is unique to her—no other royal spouse is known to have used it at any time in Egyptian history—and is always extended to specifically link her to Akhenaten. Her origins are wholly obscure; a suggestion that she might be Tadukhepa, a princess from the North Syrian state of Mitanni who had been sent to Egypt as a diplomatic bride, is interesting but without direct evidence.[18] Kiya is known from a range of monuments and objects, but in most cases they have been usurped by other persons during Akhenaten's reign: her coffin was adapted for a pharaoh's burial,[19] while most of her relief representations were recut and relabeled for Princess Meryetaten (or on occasion Ankhesenpaaten), implying disgrace.

Given that both "earlier" and "later" Aten-names were used on Kiya material, her career extended either side of Year 9/10, but as many of her monuments were usurped in the name of Meryetaten before the latter's elevation to queenship around Year 13,[20] it would seem that Kiya was disgraced well before this time (see fig. 13). Nothing in all this suggests that she might have been the mother of the heir to the throne—although she certainly bore a daughter[21]—and Kiya's candidature seems essentially to be a case of "Anyone but Nefertiti"!

Yet when one considers the ongoing tradition of not including sons in royal family depictions, the reasons for doubting that Nefertiti was the mother of Tutankhuaten become less pressing.[22] At the probable time of Tutankhuaten's birth, around Year 7/8, Nefertiti had proved her fertility by producing at least three daughters, and statistics would argue that at least one boy might have intruded into the procession of girls. A further, but equivocal, piece of evidence is that rather, later, King Ay called Tutankhamun his son. As noted later,[23] a case can be made for Nefertiti being the daughter of Ay, in which case Ay would indeed be justified in calling Tutankhamun his "(grand)son" if Nefertiti were the mother of Tutankhuaten—the future Tutankhamun. Also, when trying to reconstruct the scene from which the Ashmunein blocks derive, the fact that the two children must be facing each other is best explained through a double scene which showed Akhenaten and Nefertiti worshiping the Aten, with their children split between them. In such a context the likelihood that all the children, including Tutankhuaten, were of the same parentage seems highly likely. It of course also provides a potential family scene, of the kind whose alleged absence is such a key element of the anti-Nefertiti argument. Thus, one would suggest that in the absence of substantive evidence to the contrary, Tutankhuaten should be regarded as a child of Akhenaten and Nefertiti.

Year 12 was clearly a moment of triumph for Akhenaten, his family, and his regime. His ability to command the riches of numerous nations was combined with his ability to surround himself with a numerous family. This included his widowed mother Tiye, who seems now to have been resident at Amarna.[24] However, it has been suggested that the great *durbar*, bringing in delegations from far and wide, might have contained within it the seeds of the dynasty's downfall: plague.

A letter from the king of Alashia (almost certainly Cyprus[25]) to the king of Egypt blames his tiny gift of copper on the fact that plague had carried off all his copper workers,[26] and about fifteen years after the *durbar*, Egyptian prisoners of war taken by the Hittites infected that nation with the disease, causing widespread mortality.[27] Recent work at Amarna has indicated that in the Workmen's Village, adjacent to the city, fairly squalid conditions prevailed, with high levels of parasite infestation, in particular fleas: all in all, an ideal environment to support epidemic disease.[28] Unfortunately, it has not yet proved possible to determine whether such an epidemic disease was indeed present; however, the period following the *durbar* saw a significant number of documented deaths among the females of the royal family, contrasting with the complete lack of documented deaths during the previous decade.[29] The best attested demise is that of the king's second daughter, Meketaten.

She was buried in the innermost chamber of a suite of rooms in the tomb (TA26) that was constructed by Akhenaten in the Royal Wadi at Amarna. Unlike the earlier royal tombs in the Valley of the Kings, which were designed for a single burial—that of the king[30]—TA26 incorporated a number of subsidiary suites for royal family burials (fig. 14).[31] One suite (1–6), in many ways a miniature version of a full-size royal tomb, may have been intended for Nefertiti, while doors were marked out for two suites that were never actually constructed. The fourth comprised three rooms, two of which were decorated for burial, the innermost of which, γ, was employed for Meketaten.

The decoration of this room is wholly different from the underworld-based adornment that had been standard for burial chambers (both royal and nonroyal) of the earlier part of the Eighteenth Dynasty.[32] The end wall bears a scene of the dead princess shown as though alive, standing in a flower-draped bower; in front of her stand her mother, father, and sisters Meryetaten, Ankhesenpaaten, and Neferneferuaten-tasherit in poses of mourning (fig. 15). Behind them, and continuing on to the right-hand wall, women are shown in various poses of grief, with male mourners behind. Below them is a register showing tables and stands, laden with food and drink. The bower has been equated with a "birth pavilion"[33]: while this could well be seen as incorporating the age-old Egyptian concept of posthumous rebirth, it has also been interpreted in conjunction with the scene on the left-hand wall of chamber γ (fig. 16), which is one of the most controversial depictions in the Amarna corpus.

The focus of the scene is an image, now largely destroyed, of the body of Meketaten lying on a bier. Female mourners lament at the foot of the corpse, while at the head, the princess's parents stand together mourning their daughter. Just outside the door of the death chamber are further mourners—and a woman nursing a baby. A label-text next to the woman and baby reads "[. . .] born of [the King's Great Wife, his beloved] Neferneferu[aten]-Nefertiti, who lives for ever and eternity."

Some have seen the baby as a recently born child of Nefertiti held by a nurse (most recently Marc Gabolde has proposed that it was none other than Tutankhuaten).[34] Most, however, have concluded that the baby is a child at whose birth Meketaten has died.[35] Indeed this has become

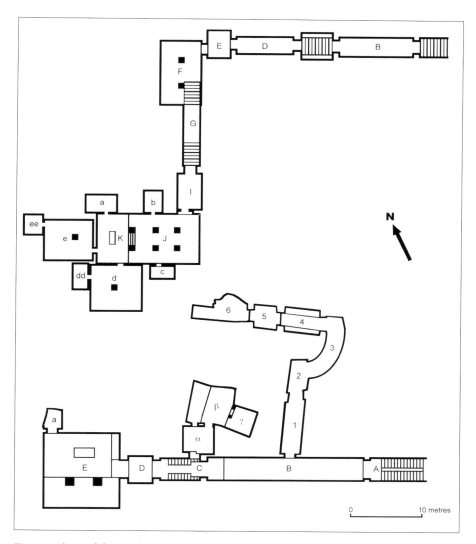

Fig. 14. Plans of the tombs of Amenhotep III (top: WV22) and Akhenaten (bottom: TA26).

one of the so-called "facts" of Amarna studies, the issue becoming the identity of the father—most presuming incest between Akhenaten and his young daughter—and whether the child survived to feature in later history. However, one must query whether or not this is really the most appropriate interpretation.

First, there is the fundamental question of whether Meketaten was old enough to have conceived a child. Although, as already noted, estimating the birth dates of the various royal children is problematic, we have the useful fact that Meketaten's figure was added as an afterthought to Boundary Stela K,[36] recording events in Year 4, and thus probably carved in Year 5. Although this could be explained as a late-rectified oversight by the sculptor, Meketaten's relatively recent birth seems the best explanation. Thus, if born in Year 4, she would have been about eight at the *durbar* and probably not even ten at her death (if we assume that her death probably took place no later than Year 14[37]). That she was both sexually active and able to conceive at that age seems highly dubious.[38]

Fig. 15. Meketaten within a bower being mourned by her parents and sisters Meryetaten, Ankhesenpaaten, and Neferneferuaten-tasherit (TA26, room γ).

Furthermore, in the other decorated chamber in the complex, room α, we find a wall that has two almost identical scenes, one above the other (fig. 17). The upper one clearly shows a child and a nurse outside the (destroyed) death chamber, but although traces of the body survive in the lower register, the area outside the room is too badly damaged to be sure whether a child was present here as well.

This double scene presumably indicates that two persons (whose names are entirely lost) were buried in room α:[39] are we therefore to assume that one or both of them also died in childbirth? While maternal mortality was certainly high, this seems a particularly excessive proportion! Also, one must question whether the cause of death really would have been indicated in

Fig. 16. Akhenaten and Nefertiti mourning the body of Meketaten. None of the figures outside the death chamber is named except for the baby in the second register, which may be the symbolically reborn Meketaten (TA26, room γ).

Fig. 17. The double death scene in TA26, room α. Virtually all label-texts are missing, so·the identity of the two dead persons is not ascertainable. The figure of a baby is again visible in the upper register, but the corresponding area in the lower register is irretrievably damaged.

such tomb-reliefs. On no other occasion in the whole of Egyptian history do we find decoration of a tomb that even hints at the cause of death; and although one can always appeal to the Amarna Period as being "different," it seems difficult to accept that such a fundamental shift would have occurred. Egyptian funerary belief was always about moving on to rebirth—the means by which one left this life was not apparently an issue. Thus, it would seem highly *un*likely that Meketaten (or the now-anonymous occupants of room α) died giving birth.[40]

So how are the "problem children" to be explained? Jacobus van Dijk has now produced a solution that may well resolve the issue.[41] He demonstrates that there is no space for anything other than the name of a child of Nefertiti in the room γ label-text, and then proposes that the name is actually that of Meketaten herself who, having died on the left of the scene, has been reborn as a babe in arms, which may even be an Amarna-style depiction of the *ka*. Thus the bower seen on the end wall may indeed refer to a birth pavilion, but one in which Meketaten is to be posthumously reborn,[42] rather than, as proposed by Geoffrey Martin, the place that witnessed her death.[43] Although van Dijk's theory does raise all sorts of further issues about the detail of Amarna funerary belief—a topic that remains obscure in many aspects[44]—this interpretation is certainly more in keeping with what we know of the generality of Egyptian funerary practices, and removes the historical and other issues that plague the received view of the scenes.

Apart from her mourning scenes, Meketaten's interment is attested with certainty only by fragments from a granite monument that was most probably her sarcophagus—the element of doubt arising from its small size and the thinness of the stone as compared to other sarcophagi in the tomb.[45] However, such reduced dimensions are consistent with a fairly small box to contain the modestly sized mummy of a juvenile.[46] It is possible that a number of small items bearing her name may derive from her funerary equipment.[47]

Who were the individuals buried in room α? To have been interred in the royal tomb would indicate they must have been members of the royal family. Evidence may be provided by a pair of very similar scenes that adorn the side walls of the room. These each show the royal family adoring the rising sun: it is unclear why this duplication occurs. On the first wall (A)[48] the king and queen were initially accompanied by Meryetaten and Meketaten, but these last two figures were later plastered over and the names of their sisters Ankhesenpaaten and Neferneferuaten-tasherit were added.[49] Presumably, images of the now four girls were carved below, but these are today lost, along with much of the plaster.[50] The figures of the king and queen have also been reworked, partly to "modernize" their appearance and also to make room for the additional princesses. At least part of the decoration of room α thus seems to date to the earlier part of Akhenaten's reign—certainly the Aten's name is in its early form—and to have been revisited when the time came to use it for a burial. In any case, the eldest four daughters seem unlikely to have been among its occupants. On the other hand, the opposite wall (C),[51] which also shows signs of rework, at one stage it named the eldest five daughters, but then had the name of Neferneferure plastered over.[52] Could this indicate that she had died and might thus be a candidate for one of the chamber's interments?[53]

While room γ was clearly decorated specifically to serve as Meketaten's burial place, this is not as immediately apparent with room α, dominated as it is by the two scenes depicting the sunrise. Indeed, the mourning scenes are awkwardly placed on the wall directly to the right of the entrance, suggesting that the allocation of room α as a burial chamber was a secondary arrangement occasioned by a premature death or deaths.[54]

There is further evidence in the tomb for the improvisation of burial arrangements. Although equipped with much more spacious corridors and stairways than earlier kings' tombs, not to mention the suites intended for royal family members, it seems that the original plans envisaged a fundamental design broadly similar to the tomb of Amenhotep III and his predecessors, with a protective shaft followed by a pillared hall, and then further galleries leading to the burial chamber. The main difference may have been that the bend in the tomb axis, found in all pre-Amarna royal tombs, was abandoned in favor of a single axis intended to allow for the theoretical penetration of the sun's rays into the burial chamber.[55]

However, apart from an abortive side chamber (Ea), the tomb was not continued beyond this pillared hall, which then had the two northern pillars removed to increase the available floor space, the area north of the surviving pillars being lowered to leave a sarcophagus plinth standing proud of the floor.[56] This would seem to indicate that a decision was made to truncate the plan of the tomb while the pillared hall (today dubbed E) was under construction, presumably in expectation of an impending interment.

That this first burial was not to be that of the king becomes apparent when one studies what is left of the decoration on the chamber walls. Although all walls are terribly damaged, in most cases making it very difficult to interpret the traces, the left wall, on what is now a raised platform behind the (now partly destroyed) pillars, is a scene in which Akhenaten, Nefertiti, and at least some of their daughters, together with a multitude of mourners, make offerings to a figure standing in a kiosk (fig. 18).

This is clearly a dead person, the whole closely paralleling the depiction of Meketaten's obsequies in room γ. The sash worn by the figure marks it as that of a queen in Amarna iconography, but it cannot be Nefertiti, since she is shown among the mourners. The only other candidate would seem

Fig. 18. Scene from the main burial chamber (E) of TA26 showing Akhenaten, Nefertiti and at least one of their daughters mourning a badly damaged female figure which may be Queen Tiye.

to be the dowager Queen Tiye.[57] This identification is supported by the presence in and around the tomb of many fragments belonging to a sarcophagus commissioned for Tiye by Akhenaten.[58] Thus it would appear that Akhenaten shared his burial chamber with his mother. Given the location of the relief along the back of the raised part of the chamber floor, it appears probable that Tiye's sarcophagus rested there, while Akhenaten's stood on the plinth in the middle of the lower section.[59] One would assume that the sarcophagus was surrounded by one or more gilded wooden shrines after the manner of the sarcophagus of Tutankhamun, given that one example made for Tiye was found in KV55[60] and would certainly have been large enough to hold the sarcophagus.

It seems likely that arrangements were made during Amenhotep III's lifetime for Tiye's potential burial in his tomb, WV22. Certainly two large chambers were added to the sepulcher, which have no previous parallels in Valley of the Kings tombs (fig. 14, Kd/e), and might be seen as prototypes for the "family suites" seen in the Amarna royal tomb. Fragmentary shabtis belonging to Tiye have been found in the tomb,[61] but it is possible that these were pre-positioned items,[62] or possibly votives at Amenhotep III's funeral,[63] and cannot count against the far more substantial material indicating Tiye's initial interment at Amarna.[64] In any case, the evidence seems fairly strong that Tiye had taken up residence at Amarna by Year 12, as the tomb of her steward, Huya (TA1), was one of those on whose walls the *durbar* was commemorated. It is, indeed, the only tomb at Amarna in which Tiye is depicted, although whether this is because of her late arrival as a resident of the city,[65] or because she did not fit in with the particular concept of royal family that dominates the other tombs in the necropolis, is a moot point.

A princess named Baketaten is seen accompanying Tiye in all the scenes in TA1.[66] In view of the close association of the two—and the fact that Baketaten's only known attestations are the examples of her as Tiye's companion[67]—the long-held view has been that she was a daughter of Tiye and Amenhotep III.[68] Some have doubted that Tiye was still able to have children at the end of her husband's life, after nearly four decades of marriage; but it is unclear how old she was on marriage, or how old Baketaten actually was when represented in TA1. She is shown as apparently the same age as Akhenaten's elder daughters, so not much more than ten years old in Year 12. However, it is important to bear in mind that she is being shown here in the role of a "King's Daughter": as such, she is almost by definition "child," and thus could actually have been a teenager or even an adult when TA1 was decorated. There are a number of cases where a person depicted as a youngster is known to have been an adult at the time the image was produced; for example, in TT64 Thutmose IV is shown as a young child— but in the company of a number of his own children![69] Thus there seems no obvious reason to doubt that Baketaten was the youngest daughter of Tiye, acting as her mother's companion, and quite possibly in her late teens or even older.[70]

While it is not possible to precisely date these various deaths in the royal family, the apparently improvised nature of the installations of Tiye and the two persons buried in room α might well suggest a flurry of deaths within a fairly short period, following on from Year 12. As we will discuss in the next chapter, there is evidence for radical measures being taken to bolster the regime in just this kind of timeframe, and thus it would seem not unlikely that the deaths should be placed in Years 13/14. They must have represented a serious blow to a regime in which the royal family as a construct played an important theological role: its very evident mortality could indeed have been feared as heralding a fundamental undermining of the whole experiment. What seems to have followed was an act of major political restructuring of a kind not previously firmly attested in pharaonic history.

2 THE WANING SUN

The construction of tombs for the nobility of Akhenaten's court began soon after Amarna was occupied, but the sheer amount of work required of the city's craftsmen meant that this work seems to have progressed in fits and starts, as and when labor could be spared. As a result, all the tombs are more or less unfinished (fig. 19). Their order of construction is not wholly clear, although the version of the Aten-name found in their decoration highlights the earlier-commenced monuments, and the number of daughters shown may have some chronological significance.[1]

However, two tombs (TA1 and TA2, of Huya and Meryre ii) stand out in each having a specifically dated relief—the *durbar* tableaux discussed in the previous chapter—which places the bulk of their decoration in or soon after Year 12. When Meryre ii's version had been carved on the right-hand wall of the principal hall of tomb-chapel, half of the hall was still undecorated. The walls on either side of the entrance had been carved—following the standard pattern seen in most unfinished tombs at Amarna and elsewhere—but the far end walls and the whole left wall were still blank. The sculptor seems to have been working clockwise round the right side of the room, so the next area to be decorated was that just to the right of the doorway that led into the inner chamber of the chapel. That the right-hand side of the chamber should have been completed first was doubtless owing to the fact that the sloping passage intended to give access to the burial chamber opened directly in front of the wall selected for the tableau of the

27

Fig. 19. The unfinished hall of the tomb-chapel of Neferkheperuhirsekheper (TA13).

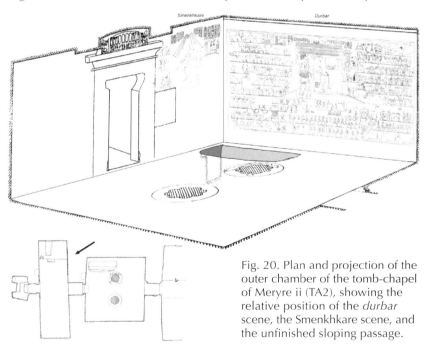

Fig. 20. Plan and projection of the outer chamber of the tomb-chapel of Meryre ii (TA2), showing the relative position of the *durbar* scene, the Smenkhkare scene, and the unfinished sloping passage.

Fig. 21. Representation of Smenkhkare and Meryetaten rewarding the tomb-owner in the tomb of Meryre ii (TA2).

durbar. Until the artists moved out of the way, the builders could not make progress in cutting the planned long corridor and chamber in which Meryre ii intended his mummy ultimately to lie (fig. 20).

Thus, the sketching out of the scene on the right-hand end wall, directly above the axis of the entrance to the sloping passage, would have been begun soon after the *durbar* scene was laid out, probably before the end of Year 12 or early in Year 13. This scene on the end wall was laid out in ink, and the carving of the upper part had begun, when the artists moved on to another job—and never returned. The scene they had been working on was a not uncommon one, of the king and queen bestowing gifts on the tomb owner. What is uncommon is the identity of the royal couple. Rather than the usual Akhenaten and Nefertiti, they are labeled as King Ankhkheperure Smenkhkare-djeserkheperu and his Great Wife, Mery(et)aten (fig. 21).[2] Meryetaten can hardly be other than Akhenaten's eldest daughter, shown only a short time previously as a mere princess, standing with her sisters behind their parents at the great *durbar*. But who was her husband and how did he fit into the history of the Amarna Period?

Smenkhkare has been perhaps the subject of even more speculation than any other individual of the period, a debate that has included matters concerning the king's very gender and/or sexuality.[3] While most substantive issues have now been overtaken by the latest research (cf. below), others still remain, in particular as regards Smenkhkare's chronological placement. Some models place his reign entirely within Akhenaten's, while others have placed it after his death. However, two key pieces of evidence make the first option by far the more probable. One is the context of Smenkhkare's depiction in TA2. As noted above, the preparation and partial carving of the scene fits well into a work schedule that began with the entrance walls and continued with the *durbar* and finally the Smenkhkare tableau, all within not much more than a year of the *durbar*'s Year 12, II *prt*, day 8. In contrast, if Smenkhkare came to the throne significantly later, the tableau's position does not fit at all with the concomitant notion of its being part of a wholly new phase of decoration. It is in a very awkward location, high on a wall directly above the meter-deep cutting of the sloping passage. Surely any new work would have been initiated somewhere in the left-hand part of the chamber, which was still devoid of decoration and ripe for new work to mark the new reign? One would thus much prefer to date the Smenkhkare tableau to Year 13/14 at the latest.

The other piece of evidence is a jar from the tomb of Tutankhamun[4] that bears an erased inscription, which for a long time was assumed to have contained the cartouches of Amenhotep III and Akhenaten together, and thus

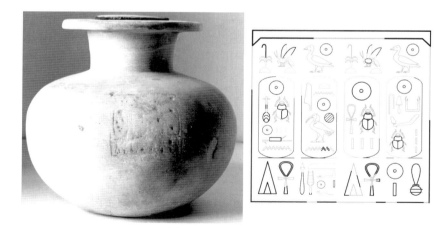

Fig. 22. Globular vase from Tutankhamun's tomb, with restoration of its erased text, giving the names of Akhenaten and Smenkhkare (Cairo JE62172).

played a role in the coregency debate. However, at length, a meticulous examination of the traces by Christian Loeben showed that the names were actually those of Akhenaten and Smenkhkare (fig. 22).[5] Although the association of two kings' names together is by no means proof that they ruled together,[6] their appearance on this kind of fairly mundane object,

Fig. 23. Ring bezels from Amarna giving the prenomen Ankhkheperure and the nomen Smenkhkare-djeserkheperu; (right: Petrie UC23801).

without any sort of formula that might suggest a memorial piece, makes this jar highly suggestive of a joint rule between Akhenaten and Smenkhkare. On the evidence of the above analysis of the TA2 representation, this is likely to have begun around Year 13/14 of Akhenaten.

Monuments of Smenkhkare are quite rare. From various parts of Amarna come ring bezels and the molds for their manufacture, as well as seal impressions (fig. 23),[7] but Smenkhkare's most impressive memorial at Amarna is a vast brick-pillared structure, which was added to the Great Palace in the center of the city (fig. 24). Built at least in

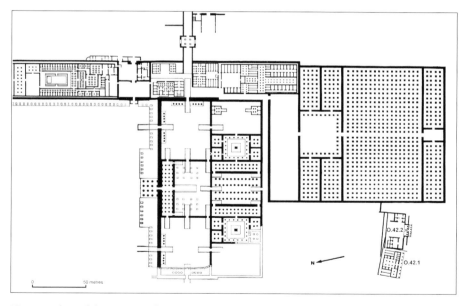

Fig. 24. Plan of the Great Palace at Amarna, with the so-called "Coronation Hall" on the right.

Fig. 25. Brick from the Coronation Hall of the Great Palace, stamped "Ankhkheperure (in) the House of Rejoicing of the Aten."

part with bricks stamped with what seems to be the building's name: "Ankhkheperure (in) the House of Rejoicing of the Aten" (fig. 25),[8] this has been dubbed the "Coronation Hall," but in fact no indication of its purpose survives. All that can be said for certain is that it was the last part of the palace to be constructed, and that it was seemingly done in a hurry.[9] Of what remains, a few fragments of painted plaster indicate that the roof of the main hall was decorated with grapes and leaves, and other parts with faience tiles;[10] a roofless room lay at the rear of the building.

The decoration would seem to indicate that the building was intended for some ceremonial purpose, as too would its clearly axial design.[11] It should be noted, however, one recent suggestion has been that it was actually a vine arbor![12] While this seems unlikely, the existence of a wine-producing estate of Smenkhkare, which continued in production after his death, is indicated by a docket on a wine jar from the first year of the reign that followed Akhenaten's,[13] which mentions an "Estate of 'Smenkhkare, [tr]ue [of voi]ce.'"[14]

Away from Amarna, a now lost block found at the ancient administrative capital of Egypt, Memphis, bears incomplete cartouches that can only be restored as those of Smenkhkare and Meryetaten, and probably once accompanied a depiction of the pair on a temple wall (fig. 26).[15] From Thebes we seem to have only a ring bezel, found at Malqata,[16] together with a decayed garment adorned with forty-seven gold daisies, each of which bore Smenkhkare's prenomen and the name of Meryetaten,[17] discovered among a bundle of miscellaneous linen items on the lion bed in Tutankhamun's tomb[18]; a linen shawl in the tomb also bore the king's prenomen.[19]

The aforementioned representation of Smenkhkare in the tomb of Meryre ii shows him beneath the protective rays of the Aten. However, the matter of Smenkhkare's religion is complicated by a graffito in the Theban tomb of Pairi (TT139),[20] dated a few years after Akhenaten's death,[21] which comprises a prayer to Amun written for a priest of Amun in the Temple of

Ankhkheperure. The implications of this will be considered further when we have looked at one of the key issues that has complicated study of the latter years of Akhenaten over the past century: the existence of a second royal titulary incorporating the name "Ankhkheperure."

An Egyptian king usually had five names, and from the Old Kingdom onwards the two most important were the so-called nomen and prenomen, both written in cartouches (see appendix 2 for those of the Amarna kings). The nomen was generally the king's birth name, sometimes supplemented by an epithet of some kind. In contrast, the prenomen, like the

Fig. 26. Lost block from Memphis, with cartouches that can only be restored as, from the right: the later-form Aten cartouches; [Ankh]kheperu[re]; [Smenkhkare-djeser]kheperu; and [Meryetaten].

Fig. 27. Amarna ring bezels giving the prenomina Ankhkheperure-mery-Neferkheperure, Ankhkheperure-mery-Waenre and, far right, Ankhetkheperure-mery-Waenre.

other three royal names, was formulated at the king's accession and specifically linked the king with the sun-god, Re. For much of Egyptian history it was usually the prenomen that was used to designate a king where the context allowed only a single name to be employed. Thus, Akhenaten was generally known as Neferkheperure, both within Egypt and in correspondence with foreign rulers.[22]

As a rule, at most periods prenomina tended to be unique, though sometimes following a similar pattern within a family group—for example, during the Eighteenth Dynasty many were of the X-kheper(u)-Re form. Occasionally an ancient one might be reused, perhaps with a distinguishing epithet—something that first became significant during the Ramesside Period when "setepenre" versus "setenpenamun" in the prenomen was enough to distinguish Usermaatre Rameses II from Usermaatre Rameses IV. This became increasingly common during the Third Intermediate Period, but during the Eighteenth Dynasty original prenomina appeared to be the universal rule. Thus, when the excavations of Flinders Petrie at Amarna revealed a more elaborate version of the Ankhkheperure cartouche, with the epithet "mery-Neferkheperure" (i.e., "beloved of Akhenaten," referred to by his prenomen),[23] it was naturally assumed to belong also to Smenkhkare (fig. 27). In such occasional usage he would be following the example of various Eighteenth Dynasty predecessors who used both simple and extended prenomina at the same time.[24]

However, in 1922, Howard Carter found in the entrance to the tomb of Tutankhamun (KV62) a piece of a box, which named together Akhenaten, King Ankhkheperure-mery-Neferkheperure Neferneferuaten-mery-Waenre, and Queen Meryetaten (fig. 28).[25] This led to the recognition that a royal name in the dateline of the aforementioned graffito in TT139 (fig. 33)[26] should be read as "Ankhkheperure-mery[. . .] Neferneferuaten-mery[. . .]," rather than "Akheperure-. . ." or even "Neferkheperure-. . .," as it had been misread by various scholars since its first publication by Urbain Bouriant in 1893, with consequent fruitless speculations.[27]

Fig. 28. Central strip of the lid of a broken box bearing the names of Akhenaten, Neferneferuaten, and Meryetaten. From the filling of the entrance stair of KV62 (Cairo JE61500a).

Given the commonality of the core "Ankhkheperure" element to both the prenomina found with "Neferneferuaten" and "Smenkhkare," it soon came to be accepted that the two names both referred to the same person. Further, it was assumed that the change between the simple and elaborate prenomina had accompanied the apparent change of nomen. As to which form came first, there was rather less unanimity. Was the king first Smenkhkare, who changed names as a sign of loyalty to Akhenaten while serving as his co-ruler, or was it a coregent Neferneferuaten who signaled a transition to sole rule by jettisoning the loyalist epithet from the prenomen and taking on a completely new nomen?[28] No one seems for a long time to have considered seriously whether there might in fact be two individuals involved.[29]

This "single individual" theory was maintained within the first challenge to the consensus in 1974. Then, in the first of a series of papers,[30] John Harris noted the existence of versions of the long prenomen that seemed to include the feminine *t*-ending (fig. 27, far right). This could be linked with a limited number of images—including a statuette found in Tutankhamun's tomb—of a king whose appearance was particularly feminine, even by Amarna art's androgynous standards (fig. 29).[31] These were in some cases juxtaposed with figures of Akhen-

Fig. 29. Statuette from KV62 of a king originally standing on the back of a black leopard; it clearly represents a woman and thus can only be an image of Neferneferuaten (Cairo JE60714).

aten in distinctly affectionate poses (e.g., fig. 32) that had led to a suspicion of a homosexual relationship between Akhenaten and Smenkhkare.[32] Harris's conclusion was that Neferneferuaten (and thus Smenkhkare) was actually a woman, and none other than Nefertiti—who had in any case borne the cognomen Neferneferuaten since Year 5. Her exceptional status while still queen consort was posited as a step toward this ultimate pharaonic status. It was additionally suggested that after Akhenaten's death she had further changed her name to Smenkhkare to mark her status as an independent ruler.

While accepted by some, this proposal was strongly opposed by others.[33] The latter camp pointed to the Meryre ii depiction and Memphis block apparently referring to a Smenkhare who was male and married, a queenly shabti of Nefertiti that could suggest she was buried as a queen, not as a (female) king,[34] and the existence of a male corpse that might well be that of Smenkhkare.[35] None of these points was easy to explain away. A middle way was proposed by Rolf Krauss in 1978, in which he suggested that while Smenkhkare/Neferneferuaten was a man, his wife Meryetaten might have ruled briefly with the feminized prenomen "Ankhetkheperure" between Akhenaten's death and her husband's accession.[36]

It was in 1988 that James P. Allen published a paper in which he proposed cutting the Gordian knot by separating Smenkhkare from Neferneferuaten, recognizing that the simple and extended versions of the Ankhkheperure cartouche could actually belong to different kings. A key observation was that there were no occasions when the extended version of the prenomen occurred alongside the nomen Smenkhkare, nor the simple prenomen with the nomen Neferneferuaten. There was by no means universal acceptance of this theory, with various scholars continuing to argue for a single male or a single female king.[37]

However, in 1998, Marc Gabolde pointed out that a number of cartouches of Neferneferuaten that had been read as having the epithet "beloved of Akhenaten" actually bore the epithet *ȝḫt n hi.s*—"effective for her husband."[38] This was confirmed beyond any doubt in 2004 by Allen and Gabolde's exhaustive reassessments of the palimpsest inscriptions on miniature gold coffins from the tomb of Tutankhamun which had contained the latter's viscera.[39] As had been recognized since at least 1940, these had originally borne the names of Neferneferuaten, but had been overwritten on reuse for Tutankhamun's burial.[40] Now it became clear that wherever the nomen's epithet could be detected on these objects, it was indeed *ȝḫt n hi.s*.[41] The femininity of Neferneferuaten was thus proven beyond doubt.

With this now firmly established, the key question remained, of course, where she came from and whether she had appeared on the monuments in a previous guise. That she was none other than Nefertiti had been the general assumption since the idea that Neferneferuaten might have been a female was first mooted, although the shadowy Kiya had on occasion been posited as a candidate for Akhenaten's female co-ruler.[42]

In theory, the discovery that one of King Neferneferuaten's epithets was "effective for her husband" left the choice between the two women open, but Kiya's unique marital status, her early disappearance from the scene, and the erasure of her figures from her monuments all militate against her. However, there can be no question that Nefertiti was Akhenaten's spouse *par excellence*—and that since Year 5 her full name had actually been Neferneferuaten-Nefertiti. In addition, her standing as queen had been exceptional throughout the reign, going so far on occasion as to have her represented in kingly pose, smiting a cowering enemy (fig. 30).[43]

In spite of the apparently open and shut nature of this case, two other candidates for Neferneferu-

Fig. 30. Nefertiti smiting an enemy, as shown on the exterior of the cabin of her state barge; this parallels a similar depiction on Akhenaten's barge in the same relief. From Ashmunein (MFA 64.521).

aten's original identity have been put forward, from among the daughters of Akhenaten and Nefertiti. The more popular has been Meryetaten,[44] but the aforementioned box fragment from the tomb of Tutankhamun naming together King Akhenaten, King Neferneferuaten, and Queen Meryetaten requires some rather tortured logic to make the last two the same person! A further candidate has been Akhenaten and Nefertiti's fourth daughter Neferneferuaten-tasherit.[45] However, her name appears to be the most positive factor in her favor, given that at the time King Neferneferuaten seems to appear in the record, Neferneferuaten-tasherit can have been, at most, around ten years old, with two of her elder sisters—Meryetaten and Ankhesenpaaten—not to mention the Prince Tutankhuaten, still alive. In such circumstances, it is difficult to maintain a convincing argument as to why she should have been elevated to kingship above her siblings—or given the epithet "effective for her husband" without her ever having been a king's wife.[46] We will return to the *raison d'être* of the appointment of Smenkhkare and Neferneferuaten later.

In connection with these other suggestions, evidence has been put forward that Nefertiti must have died a mere queen, and thus cannot have survived to become a king. One piece of evidence cited has been the existence of a broken shabti-figure bearing Nefertiti's queenly name and titles.[47] However, like all ancient Egyptians of rank, Nefertiti will certainly have had her principal items of funerary equipment made long before she could have contemplated ending life as a king. The "problem shabti" should most likely be seen as strayed from some palace storeroom, abandoned at Nefertiti's change of status, rather than from her burial.

Thus the most credible reconstruction would seem to be that Queen Neferneferuaten-Nefertiti and King Neferneferuaten were one and the same, and followed Smenkhkare as Akhenaten's coregent (chart 1). That the configuration of the royal family was rather curious is suggested by the KV62 box fragment that has already been referred to more than once. How is one to regard Meryetaten's title of "King's Great Wife" on this piece? Does the title relate to her status as the relict of Smenkhkare, or as "wife" of her father—or perhaps even her mother as well? It is clear that the title Great Wife was not simply a designation of the king's senior sexual partner. Rather, she had key ritual roles, and it is to fulfil these functions that we have cases of a father "espousing" his daughters (like Rameses II) or even—in this potential case—a mother having her daughter as her "wife." That Meryetaten remained an important figure after the death of her husband is indicated by the fact that Burnaburiash of Babylon sent her gifts,[48] and that she seems to have been particularly highly regarded by Abimilki of Tyre.[49]

We now return to the question of the identity of Smenkhkare.[50] Under normal circumstances one would expect a coregent to be the eldest son of the senior king, acting as a "staff of old age," as the Egyptians put it. In the past a large number of coregencies have been posited throughout Egyptian history,[51] although there has been a trend to doubt many of them, including even the apparently securely double-dated Twelfth Dynasty ones.[52] Nevertheless, the very fact that coregency bestowed pharaonic status on an individual would strongly imply that the person in question should be in the line of succession. In this connection, even Hatshepsut felt the need to claim formal nomination as Thutmose I's successor to justify her self-elevation to coregency with Thutmose III.

Thus one could certainly take the view that Smenkhkare was Akhenaten's elder son, perhaps a year older or younger than his sister-wife, Meryetaten. However, in Year 13/14 he would have been only twelve or so and no more than fifteen (and presumably dead) when replaced as coregent by Neferneferuaten before the end of Akhenaten's reign. This sits uncomfortably with the twenty or more years of age assessed for a body that, as we shall see, seems most likely to be that of Smenkhkare,[53] and thus would argue against Smenkhkare being Akhenaten's son.

If Smenkhkare was *not* Akhenaten's son, why then was he elevated to kingship ahead of Tutankhuaten, who *was* by all appearances Akhenaten's son and thus heir apparent to the throne? The answer may well lie in the identity of the person who followed Smenkhkare in the coregency: Nefertiti, who, royal by marriage only, can never have been in the line of succession.

We have already raised the possibility that the deaths of Meketaten, Tiye, and perhaps other members of the royal family were due to epidemic disease around Year 13/14, the very time that Smenkhkare seems to appear on the scene. One wonders if, against this background, Akhenaten decided that some guarantee of his regime's continuity was needed: his own lifespan might become attenuated, and he was aware that the bureaucratic elite did not necessarily wholeheartedly support his reforms. Thus he appointed in succession two adults who, ideally, could do one of two things. They could smooth the accession of Tutankhuaten and act as Tutankhuaten's own coregent, at least until he reached his majority. Or, if Tutankhuaten were also to be carried off, they would be able (given that the direct male line was now extinct) to ensure their own continuation as substantive king from the position of authority of an anointed pharaoh. Both options would thus guarantee the continuation of Akhenaten's revolution.

In this case the choice of coregent was a matter of the most suitable adult, rather than the next in line for the throne—although clearly membership of the royal family would be a factor. Against this background Nefertiti, as Great Wife and probably mother of the heir to the throne, was an ideal candidate. But why then would Smenkhkare be appointed in advance of her? Part of the reason was doubtless the view that a male would be more effective in the role: ancient Egypt was, after all, a patriarchal society, albeit perhaps more liberal as regards female roles than some ancient states. It is also possible that Smenkhkare was heir presumptive after Tutankhuaten: Smenkhkare's putative body is certainly that of a close relative of Tutankhuaten,[54] and as regards age, would fit nicely as a younger brother of Akhenaten.

We thus have a scenario that, in the wake of the post-Year 12 deaths, Smenkhkare was married to Meryetaten and set up as coregent. However, his reign was short and within a year or two he was himself dead—perhaps a victim of the disease he was meant to be guarantor against. Whether his marriage to Meryetaten produced offspring is unclear, although at twelve or thirteen she will have been just about old enough to bear children. A child named Meryetaten-tasherit, known from Amarna blocks found at Ashmunein,[55] has often been identified as Meryetaten's on the basis of her name. This individual appears on these blocks[56] both explicitly and implicitly, in cases where only the "-tasherit" element remains along with a further girl, Ankhesenpaaten-tasherit. It is clear that at least one of these girls was a granddaughter of (presumably) Nefertiti, as a block from Karnak preserves what was clearly once part of an inscription reading "[. . .-ta]sherit, born of [. . .] born of the King's Great Wife [. . .]."[57]

Interpretation is hampered by the incomplete state of the inscriptions and the fact that at least some of the texts involved have been cut over inscriptions referring to Kiya and her daughter. Some scholars have thus taken the view that Meryetaten-tasherit and Ankhesenpaaten-tasherit might be Kiya's children, or even phantoms conjured up to fill in the gaps caused by the erasure of Kiya's inscriptions![58] Indeed, this may have led to some distortions, as renaming a figure of Kiya for Ankhesenpaaten or (more usually) Meryetaten when that figure was accompanied by Kiya's daughter might make it appear that the said princess had become a mother when this was not actually the case. On the other hand, it does seem difficult to doubt that Meryetaten-tasherit and Ankhesenpaaten-tasherit actually existed: the question is who were their mother(s) and father(s)?

The majority view has been that Meryetaten-tasherit and Ankhesenpaaten-tasherit were the offspring of Meryetaten and Ankhesenpaaten, respectively, and that the father was Akhenaten. The latter aspect has doubtless been influenced, if only implicitly, by Akhenaten's alleged paternity of "Meketaten's baby." However, given that this baby seems likely not to have existed,[59] there is actually no solid evidence for any of Akhenaten's daughters giving birth while holding no higher title than King's Daughter. Perhaps the most straightforward solution is that Meryetaten-tasherit and Ankhesenpaaten-tasherit were the children of Smenkhkare and Meryetaten, making them the offspring of a married couple,[60] named after the mother and her surviving younger sister.

We now need to return to the question of the fate of Smenkhkare's body, which raises a number of issues, ultimately tied to an evaluation of the contents of a tomb found in the Valley of the Kings at Thebes in 1907.[61] Now known as KV55, this contained a range of material including a mutilated funerary shrine of Queen Tiye, a set of canopic jars that had originally been made for Kiya, and a coffin made for her prior to Year 12—on the basis of the early form of the Aten's names—reworked for a now nameless king,[62] and containing a mummy. This body has been examined on a number of occasions with varying results, but there is a broad consensus that the individual was in his twenties at the time of his death.[63] This is generally regarded as too young to be Akhenaten who, one would assume was at least out of his teens when he founded Akhet-Aten—given that his parents had been married for nearly four decades when he came to the throne, he could have been considerably older.[64] This leaves Smenkhkare as apparently the only credible candidate.

So why might Smenkhkare have ended up in the coffin? An answer may be found in the tomb of Tutankhamun, where the middle coffin of the nest of three that held his mummy differs from the other two very considerably. First, in contrast to the chased, plain gold surfaces seen on these other coffins, the middle coffin is heavily inlaid with colored glass, a feature only found on the KV55 coffin and fragments found in the tomb of Amenhotep III.[65] Second, the face bears little resemblance to other depictions of Tutankhamun, being much squarer and almost certainly representing a different individual (fig. 31). Furthermore, close inspection shows that the interiors of cartouches on the coffin lid are sunk below the level of the gilded background to the rest of the texts, and are perhaps less carefully crafted. That both nomen and prenomen cartouches are involved shows that any cartouche replacement cannot have been simply the result of the king's name-change from Tutankh*aten* to Tutankh*amun*.[66] A further point regarding the coffin is the fact that a medical artist's 1966 blind reconstruction of the face of the KV55 mummy looks uncannily like the visage of the middle coffin.[67] While the uncertainties regarding such reconstructions make this clearly not a decisive piece of evidence, it is certainly useful supporting evidence.

If this apparent coffin of Smenkhkare was ultimately used for Tutankhamun, why was he himself not buried in it? The clue may lie in its texts: it is entirely traditional in its formulations, contrasting radically with the KV55 coffin. This possible traditionalism on the part of Smenkhkare has been mentioned earlier in relation to the Temple of Amun in the Temple of Ankhkheperure that existed some years after his death.[68] One wonders if such a traditional coffin was regarded as unacceptable by Akhenaten,[69] who

Fig. 31. Face of the coffin used as the middle element in the coffin nest of Tutankhamun, but probably made for Smenkhkare—and thus perhaps the only surviving portrait of the latter king. From KV62 (Cairo JE60670).

instead substituted, for Smenkhkare's interment, a "religiously correct" coffin originally made for the now disgraced Kiya.[70] As to where the coffin and its contents were laid to rest, it is possible that it could have been placed somewhere in the increasingly crowded royal tomb—perhaps in room β or somewhere in the 1-6 complex—or perhaps in tomb TA28, a multi-chambered sepulcher in the southern branch of the Royal Wadi which may have been intended for the overspill from the royal tomb itself. We will return to KV55 in Chapter 4.

King Neferneferuaten's appointment as Smenkhkare's replacement may not initially have included an investiture with a full pharaonic titulary. One stela (fig. 32) has a scene that should almost certainly be seen as showing Akhenaten and a blue-crown-wearing Nefertiti/Neferneferuaten, but with only three (empty) cartouches for the rulers' names. A similar situation may have existed on a fragmentary stela (fig. 33).[71] Here the cartouche and title of Nefertiti has been erased and replaced by her prenomen, her nomen being squeezed into the gap between the prenomen and the border of the stela at the expense of the name of Meryetaten which had previously been there.[72] Unfortunately the stela is so badly damaged that it is very difficult to be clear as to either the original design or how its figures might have been amended to match the change in the texts,[73] in particular whether the figure of Nefertiti had worn a king's crown in either version of the stela's royal images.

Fig. 32. Unfinished stela of Pay, apparently showing Akhenaten (on the right, given the double crown?) and Neferneferuaten (on the left, given the femininity of the breasts?); both figures are seemingly naked. As only three cartouches are provided for the kings, the stela must date between the death of Smenkhkare and a possibly delayed adoption of a prenomen by the former Nefertiti. From Amarna (Berlin 17813).

Apart from these pieces, it is difficult to identify many objects that can definitely be dated to the period of Akhenaten and Neferneferuaten's period of co-rule. It is likely that various examples of the afore-mentioned ring bezels, etc., belong to this period, but one cannot be certain. Remains of painted plaster bearing Neferneferuaten's kingly cartouches in the North Riverside Palace suggest her residence there,[74] but nothing indicates whether it dates before or after Akhenaten's death. The house of the chariotry officer Ranefer (N49.18, in the Main City South) was certainly rebuilt during Nefer-neferuaten's time, its limestone doorframe being inscribed with her names.[75] It is not possible to say exactly when Neferneferuaten became coregent, other than to make a broad assumption that her appointment closely followed Smenkhkare's death—perhaps in Year 14/15. The further question is then how long she remained king, which brings in one of the most important records of the period: a modest graffito in an old tomb-chapel, but one that has some potentially far-reaching implications.

This text, already twice noted above, is to be found in the tomb of Pairi (TT139), which dates to the reign of Amenhotep III and is of very simple form.[76]

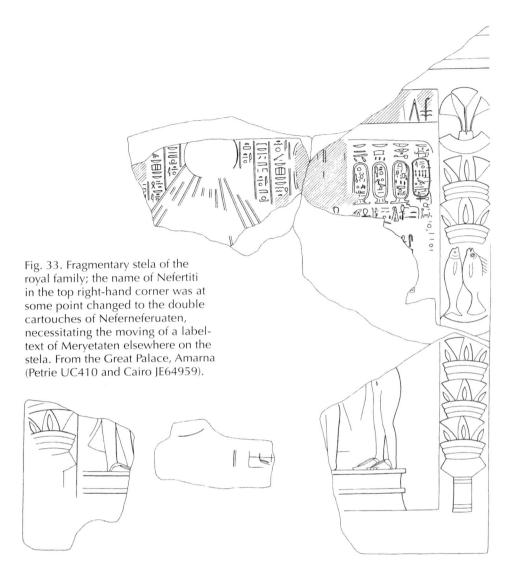

Fig. 33. Fragmentary stela of the royal family; the name of Nefertiti in the top right-hand corner was at some point changed to the double cartouches of Neferneferuaten, necessitating the moving of a label-text of Meryetaten elsewhere on the stela. From the Great Palace, Amarna (Petrie UC410 and Cairo JE64959).

Over the doorway leading to the burial passage in the far right-hand corner of its single chamber a draftsman named Ba(?)tjay wrote in hieratic script a prayer to Amun on behalf of his blind brother, the *waab*-Priest and Scribe of Divine Offerings of Amun, Pawah (fig. 34). Batjay and Pawah were both on the staff of the Temple of Ankhkheperure. As noted above (pp. 32–33), this name employs the simple form of that prenomen, with the implication that the king referred to is Smenkhkare, thus linking Akhenaten's first coregent very much with the cult of Amun.

But it is the dateline that has particularly gripped scholars, since it places the writing of the graffito on day 3 of IV *prt* in Year 3 of "Ankhkheperure-mery-[. . .] Neferneferuaten-meryet[77]-[. . .]." This is the only unequivocal date in Neferneferuaten's reign, and the key question has been whether it forms part of a sequence begun on her appointment as coregent or one begun on her accession to non-dependent rule. The question of double-dating during New Kingdom coregencies is even more controversial than in the Middle Kingdom, with no unequivocal examples being known.[78] On this basis—and given our assumptions on the putative motivation behind Neferneferuaten's elevation to pharaonic status—it would seem unlikely that Neferneferuaten will have started counting regnal years until after Akhenaten's death. This is supported by the existence of a jar docket from Amarna that has "Year 1" written over "Year 17,"[79] implying that a new enumeration of regnal years began only after Akhenaten's death.

But was she counting just her own years? It seems far more likely that Neferneferuaten transitioned from being Akhenaten's coregent, implicitly using his regnal years, to being the coregent of King Nebkheperure Tutankhaten, sharing the new king's regnal years in the same way. This would of course be the fulfilment of precisely the scenario we envisaged behind the successive appointment to coregency of Smenkhkare and Neferneferuaten. Potential support for the co-rule of Tutankhaten and Neferneferuaten is provided by the fact that at Tell el-Borg in Sinai was found a group of jar handles which together bore stamps of each

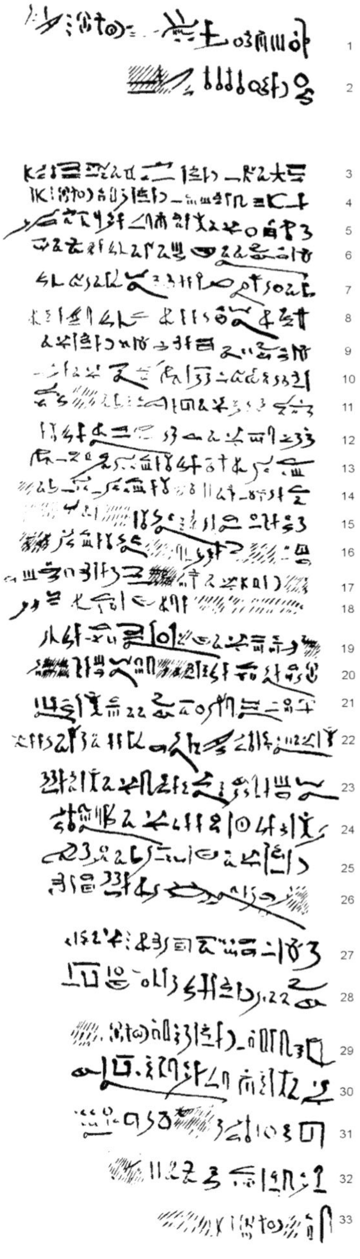

Fig. 34. Graffito of Pawah in the tomb of Pairi on Sheikh Abd el-Qurna (TT139).

of her cartouches (the nomen with the epithet *ꜣḫt n ḥi.s*) as well as others with Tutankhaten's prenomen.[80] A fragment of relief from the same site may represent one or more of these kings.[81]

That Akhenaten's appointment of Neferneferuaten as a putative guarantee of an Atenist future beyond his lifetime may have been fatally flawed is indicated by the content of the TT139 graffito. It shows that within three years of Akhenaten's death, Amun establishments were functioning fully once again. Intriguing questions are also raised by the existence of this Temple of Ankhkheperure: was it a mortuary establishment founded during Smenkhkare's short coregency, or something brought into existence following Akhenaten's death? Or might it, like the later "Temple of Nebkheperure," have been at Karnak?[82]

It is also unclear precisely what Neferneferuaten was calling herself at this time. The epithets of both prenomen and nomen in the TT139 graffito are damaged and/or problematic, but the first certainly does not contain part of Akhenaten's prenomen—instead possibly a divine name beginning with *ỉ*. The nomen could conceivably end with "meryet-Waenre," as was originally suggested,[83] but only some kind of horizontal sign is certain, and the final word might also begin with an *ỉ*.[84] One or both could thus have been a simple "meryetaten"—or conceivably even "meryetamun"! In favor of the former for the prenomen is the existence of some three gold sequins bearing this version, together with the nomen "Neferneferuaten-heqa."[85] Altogether there seem to be at least five different combinations of epithets employed in Neferneferuaten's cartouches (appendix 2).

Thus we have the apparently incongruous scenario of Akhenaten's wife and apparent fellow prime mover of the Aten revolution overseeing its unpicking and a return to orthodoxy—or at least to a more pantheist view in which Amun was once again acceptable. How long, then, had Amun been unacceptable?

If the aforementioned Amun foundation of Smenkhkare was indeed established during Smenkhkare's own brief period of rule, and this is to be dated around Year 13/14 of Akhenaten, it could be highly significant in relation to the dating of the persecution of Amun. Opinion has long been divided between those who would have the persecution take place soon after the move to Amarna, and those who would put it in the very last years of Akhenaten. Among more recent writers, Susanne Bickel has argued[86] that the proscription of Amun should be placed in or soon after Year 5.[87] However, it should be pointed out that Amun's consort, Mut, was still sufficiently regarded that her vulture could be inscribed, as part of the name of

Nefertiti's sister Mutnodjmet,[88] in a number of Amarna tombs carved between Year 5 and the change in the name of the Aten between Years 8 and 12. In at least one case the Mut vulture was apparently later erased, but in another three it remained intact.[89] In addition, the door of the funerary shrine of Queen Tiye—which bears the later form of the Aten's names—had her late husband's full nomen "Amenhotep" inscribed on it, although the "Amun" element was later erased.[90] In addition, Tiye's sarcophagus, also a later piece, has the figure of Maat carved in some cases, although spelled out in others.[91]

This would suggest that the proscription of Amun must be pushed later than the change in the Aten's names, an event that has been regarded by some as a possible trigger for the persecution. If an Amun institution was founded during the coregency of Smenkhkare, a dating of the persecution to after his death becomes an attractive option. Indeed, there is much to be said for placing it in the very last year or so of Akhenaten's reign: although violent and comprehensive, the persecution was restricted to mutilating inscriptions and divine images. One would have thought the erasure of the Karnak deities' names and figures would have been but a precursor to the demolition of their sanctuaries. However, there is no evidence for this happening, which surely would have been the logical outcome of an early-onset persecution, against the background of the increasingly austere monotheism indicated by the change of the Aten name. Likewise, no other gods outside the Theban triad seem to have been affected by direct action,[92] although the retrospective Restoration Stela of Tutankhamun[93] suggests that non-Aten sanctuaries may have been starved of resources.[94] One thus tends toward Cyril Aldred's old view that far from reflecting the beginning of the revolution, the persecution of Amun represented its last gasp, "the last great act of Akhenaten's reign [reflecting] a mental collapse on the part of its author."[95] Whether it also triggered currently unknowable events that ended both his reign and life remains a matter for speculation.

However Akhenaten's life ended, it would appear, as we have seen, that Neferneferuaten continued in power, only now accompanied by a new co-ruler, King Nebkheperure Tutankhaten.[96] That Akhenaten was given a full pharaonic funeral in the royal tomb is all but certain, given the important role that the carrying out of the burial played in the transmission of an inheritance from one generation to the next.[97] Claims that (e.g.) the unstained state of the canopic chest of Akhenaten might suggest it had not been anointed with unguents, and thus not used, are highly subjective[98] and do not constitute substantive reasons for doubting that the burial took place. Much data was subsequently lost when most of the funerary equipment—including the granite sarcophagus—was smashed to smithereens (fig. 35).

Tutankhaten was married to his sister Ankhesenpaaten, and the royal couple are shown together, beneath the rays of the Aten, on the back of a lavish gilded and inlaid throne (fig. 36);[99] another inscribed chair also linked the king with the Aten.[100] However, on a small stela that was apparently found at Amarna (fig. 37),[101] the new king is shown offering to none other than Amun and Mut: taken together, an attempt at triangulating a religious line that embraced the old and the new seems apparent.

There is also some data on the continued upbringing of the king. We have already seen the links between the family of Queen Tiye and the city of Akhmim. Interestingly, a tomb-chapel across the river at Awlad Azzaz was made for a certain Sennedjem, who lived into Tutankhamun's reign, when his tomb was constructed.[102] His principal title was Overseer of Tutors, and his status was further emphasized by his being Fanbearer on the Right of the King, a Noble, and a Count. Since he also included an image of Tutankhamun in his tomb, it seems likely that he was indeed one of those charged with bringing up the prince.[103] A female nurse is also known, from a tomb-chapel at Saqqara whose owner, Lady Maya, included

Fig. 35. The sarcophagus of Akhenaten, restored from fragments; Nefertiti is shown on the corners in the guise of a protective goddess (Cairo TR 3/3/70/2).

in its decoration a scene of the king sitting on her lap (fig. 38).[104] In both cases, the king is given the later form of his name, but as such monuments are clearly retrospective,[105] it is unclear whether Sennedjem and Maya's ministrations date from the later part of the king's childhood, the early years of his reign, his life prior to Akhenaten's death, or a number of these eras.

It seems fairly clear that the elder coregent Neferneferuaten's intention was to maintain Amarna as a key royal residence. Ring bezels are found there bearing the names of the king and his wife in various parts of the city, in particular from the Workmen's Village, where sixty percent of such items are named Tutankhaten.[106] Only six percent referred to Neferneferuaten, suggesting that, at least nominally, Tutankhaten was the senior ruler. Jar labels dated from Years 1 to 4— which must belong to the new regime, as the city was only occupied from Akhenaten's Year 5— indicate continuing court activity at Amarna, although it is interesting that while Years 1 and 2 are fairly well represented, Years 3 and 4 are much less so, suggesting an increasing emphasis on older centers such as Memphis and Thebes as time went by.[107]

Fig. 36. The back of the throne from KV62, showing Tutankhaten and Ankhesenpaaten in the Amarna style, under the rays of the Aten. The king's and queen's cartouches have here been altered from to their Amun-forms but elsewhere on the throne, with one exception, they remain in their original, Atenist, forms (Cairo JE62028).

Fig. 37. Stela showing Tutankhaten offering to Amun and Mut. Apparently from Amarna (Berlin 14197).

It has been assumed that the aforementioned Workmen's Village was associated with construction work in the Royal Wadi,[108] in which case it is interesting that the majority of royal names found there are from

Fig. 38. Partly destroyed relief in tomb I.20 at the Bubastaeon at Saqqara, showing Tutankhamun on the lap of his nurse, Maya.

the end of the period of Amarna's existence as a capital city. In any case, one must assume that Smenkhkare, Neferneferuaten, and Tutankhaten had planned to be buried there. Certainly two of the unfinished tombs in the southern branch of the Royal Wadi (see fig. 39 and map 2) have every appearance of having been intended as kingly ones, with a third (TA30)—opposite TA26 in the original branch—so incomplete that it is difficult to form an opinion.[109] One, TA27, comprises most of the first corridor, penetrating no more than thirteen meters into the rock. In contrast, TA29 was no less than forty-five meters long when work was terminated, partway down to what would have been a stairway, following on from three full corridors (fig. 40).

As to exactly who had begun each of these tombs there is no direct evidence. As noted earlier, if Smenkhkare had begun a tomb at Amarna, it would presumably have been in this area, but given his short reign it is unlikely to have proceeded far, and may have been continued by a successor. Tomb TA29 could be attributed to Neferneferuaten, co-ruler at Amarna for an aggregate of some five or six years, and TA27 to Tutankhaten, but whichever tomb was intended as hers, Neferneferuaten had certainly begun the manufacture of the customary funerary equipment of a pharaoh. These included the coffinettes for her viscera,[110] mummy-trappings,[111] a bow,[112] a box,[113] bracelets,[114] and a pectoral (fig. 41),[115] all of which were later reworked to a greater or lesser degree for use in Tutankhamun's burial.[116] It is also possible that the sarcophagus ultimately used for Tutankhamun was begun for Neferneferuaten, as it underwent a major reworking during its manufacturing history.[117]

As regards the policy pursued by this regime, one can probably infer from the TT139 graffito, and the aforementioned stela of Tutankhaten before Amun and Mut, a gradual stepping back from Akhenaten's religious policy, with a re-establishment of Amun-worship and probably a restoration

Fig. 39. South branch in the Royal Wadi that appears to have been the intended burial place of Neferneferuaten and Tutankhaten.

of resources to non-Aten sanctuaries. This distancing from Akhenaten may also be seen in the form of Neferneferuaten's names in use by Year 3. While this might on the face of it appear a remarkable *volte face* by a woman who had for so long been such an integral part of the whole Amarna experiment, history is replete with examples of such dramatic repositionings, as apparently principled individuals rapidly adjust themselves to political reality! Also, although now apparently accepting the old cults, her continued attachment to the Aten itself is indicated by the maintenance of the "-aten" elements in the royal names.

The TT139 graffito is, however, our last certain glimpse of Neferneferuaten. As to whether she died or was otherwise removed from the scene soon after Year 3, no unequivocal evidence exists. However, it is clear that her meticulously prepared funerary equipment was

Fig. 40. Tomb TA29 in the Royal Wadi at Amarna.

Fig. 41. Pectoral originally made for Neferneferuaten, whose names are clearly visible under those of Tutankhamun. From KV62 (Cairo JE61944).

not used for her funeral, as many items from it were used within a few years for the burial of Tutankhamun. This suggests that if she died at this time, she certainly was not buried as a king.[118]

The implication must therefore be that Neferneferuaten either died and was posthumously denied her kingly status, or was deposed—while recognizing that these options need not be exclusive. Her disappearance from the scene is likely to have been the cue for the next phase in the post-Akhenaten counter-reformation. During these early years, Neferneferuaten and Tutankhaten had retained their Atenist names. The same was true of Ankhesenpaaten. It is likely that it was with Neferneferuaten's disappearance from the scene that the young couple's new guardians induced the change of their names to Tutankhamun and Ankhesenamun, and the explicit return to full orthodoxy began.

3 THE NORTHERN PROBLEM

During the internally momentous years of Akhenaten's reign Egypt was one of the great powers of the ancient world and a key node in a complex of diplomatic links. As such, it was the pharaoh's role to correspond both with his fellow monarchs—an exclusive band that called each other "brother" (appendix 1)[1]—together with a large swath of vassal princes of Syria-Palestine. The latter were an inheritance from the conquests of the earlier kings of the Eighteenth Dynasty, in particular Thutmose III (map 3).[2] There is no direct evidence for any campaigning in this area under Akhenaten,[3] although some of the Amarna correspondence could imply an Egyptian attack on Qadesh, the key city in northern Syria, late in his reign.[4]

A considerable amount of data for the reconstruction of these relationships during the late fourteenth century BC is provided by two groups of cuneiform tablets. The first is the Amarna Letters, a group of cuneiform tablets found at that site in 1887 (and a few subsequently). They comprised communications between the rulers of the various states of the Near East and kings Amenhotep III, Akhenaten, and Tutankhamun.[5] The second group derives from the Hittite archives at Boğazkale (Boğazköy) in Anatolia, in particular those comprising the "Deeds of Shuppiluliumash," written in the time of his son, Murshilish II, and forming an introduction to that king's "Plague Prayers."[6] Some fragmentary letters also survive.

The Hittite material is important because a key motif of the period covered by this book is the steady expansion of Hittite power in northern

Syria, through which the Hittites came into conflict both with the kingdom of Mitanni—for the past few decades an Egyptian ally—and with Egypt itself over the loyalty of their vassals in the region. The precise chronology of what happened and when is difficult to assess from the surviving documentation, with a number of different reconstructions put forward by modern researchers.

However, the key figure is the Hittite king Shuppiluliumash I, who seized the throne shortly before Akhenaten's accession.[7] After some time spent consolidating his power in Anatolia, he began to flex his muscles to the south. An attack on Mitanni was repulsed by its king, Tushratta, who sent a tithe of material captured from the Hittites as a gift to Amenhotep III.[8] However, this was followed up by Shuppiluliumash's "Great Syrian War," the justification for which was probably provided by an attack by Tushratta on Hatti's north Syrian ally, Nukhashshe; this was accompanied by an uprising in the nearby state of Isuwa. Shuppiluliumash crossed the Euphrates, conquered Isuwa and entered Mitanni. Tushratta failed to offer battle, as a result of which his capital Washshukanni was occupied and sacked. The Hittites then turned west and took control of all the various Mitannian vassal cities in northern Syria. In addition, Qadesh, which had previously owed allegiance to Egypt, was also taken into the Hittite sphere after its ruler had foolishly attempted to attack Shuppiluliumash's forces.

Another Egyptian ally in the area was the land of Amurru, with a considerable population of seminomadic warlike tribes known as the Apiru.[9]

These have on occasion been equated with the Hebrews, but this has been purely on the basis of the similarity of the name. Using Apiru troops, a certain Abdiashirta had become ruler of Amurru some years previously and was busy expanding his influence. This alarmed another Egyptian ally, Ribaddi of Byblos (Gubla) on the Lebanese coast. Byblos had had strong links with Egypt since the Old Kingdom, and was an important trading port, in particular being the center of the export trade in cedar, a vital commodity for Egypt, which lacked good quality native woods.

Ribaddi wrote repeatedly to Egypt reporting Abdiashirta's aggressive takeover of neighboring cities and calling on the Egyptian king to intervene. However, Abdiashirta represented himself to the pharaoh as a loyal vassal of Egypt working closely with the Egyptian Resident Pahunnate (Egyptian: Pahemnetjer), and clearly the Egyptian government took the view that this was a local issue and, provided the territory remained aligned to Egypt, there was little reason to intervene. Byblos was seemingly about to be added to Abdiashirta's kingdom when Abdiashirta himself suddenly died—whether naturally or by violence is unknown.

His son and successor, Aziru, soon resumed Abdiashirta's expansionist policy, once again writing frequently to Akhenaten in the guise of a loyal servant of the Egyptian crown, and complaining that local Egyptian officials were obstructing his activities. He warned, however, of fears regarding the Hittites, and requested military aid from Egypt in the event of a Hittite attack.[10] However, when at last Byblos fell into Aziru's hands, and the latter allied with the King of Qadesh—of course now a Hittite vassal—Aziru was summoned to Egypt, where he was detained for a year.

Thus, although at this stage there seems not to have been a direct attack by the Hittites on Egyptian possessions, most of their north Syrian client states had begun to pass under Shuppiluliumash's suzerainty during the latter part of Akhenaten's reign and into the first part of Tutankhaten's. Such a "cold war" between the two states may be suggested by the tone of a letter written by Shuppiluliumash to a king "Khuria" of Egypt on the latter's accession:[11]

> Why, my brother, have you held back the presents that your father made to me when he was alive? Now you, my brother, have ascended the throne of your father, and, just as your father and I were desirous of peace between us, so now too should you and I be friendly with one another (*trans.* after Moran).

The identity of the recipient is made obscure by the fact that the Hittite scribe has seemingly attenuated the Egyptian king's name. At this time, the normal way of referring to a pharaoh was by his prenomen, and this convention was followed by his overseas correspondents, albeit transcribed into Akkadian. So Thutmose III (Menkheperre) appeared as "Manakhpiya," Amenhotep III (Nebmaatre) as "Nibmuariya," Akhenaten (Neferkheperure) as "Napkhuriya" and Tutankhamun (Nebkheperure) as "Nibkhuriya." Thus, Shuppiluliumash was writing to a king whose prenomen was clearly "X-kheperure," but with the first element omitted.

Four kings fit this pattern: Akhenaten, Smenkhkare, Neferneferuaten, and Tutankhamun. The second can be ruled out: Smenkhkare seems never to have reigned alone, as is demanded by the contents. Arguments can be made for Akhenaten being the recipient, but the tone of the letter fits better with the aftermath of the great Syrian campaign and the ongoing

Fig. 42. The tomb built by Horemheb at Saqqara prior to his accession as king.

events in Amurru. It was thus most probably sent to Egypt after the death of Akhenaten, to be received by the co-rulers Neferneferuaten and Tutankhaten. The letter's address to the Hittite king's "brother" would seemingly suggest that the intended addressee was not the female Neferneferuaten; on the other hand, diplomacy may have deemed her to be technically male—and certainly "Khuria" could be taken as a contraction of "Ankhkheperure," the Hittite ear conflating the two *h*-sounds at the beginning of the name. Or did the existence of two kings lead to confusion in Hatti, resulting in the use of a neutral "Khuriya"?

"Hot war" seems to have followed soon afterward, however: in Aziru's absence cities in Amqa (the Beqaa Valley), within Egypt's sphere of influence, had been taken over by the Hittites and a large band of Hittite troops had massed in Nukhashshe, suggesting a planned attack on Amurru. Aziru was allowed to return, but not long afterward threw off his long-professed loyalty to Egypt and threw in his lot with the Hittites, agreeing a treaty with Shuppiluliumash. This low point in Egyptian fortunes in the area may well be reflected in a monumental text, bemoaning the country's impotence in Syrian affairs, which was apparently produced around Year 4 of Tutankhamun.[12]

Documentation is sparse for the next few years, but that the Egyptians made some attempt to regain the initiative is suggested by a number of depictions from Tutankhamun's reign. In the tomb of General Horemheb (later to become king) at Saqqara (figs. 42, 62, and 79)[13] are to be found scenes that show the presentation of a range of captives from Syria[14]— including Hittites—together with a delegation from the region requesting terms (figs. 43 and 44).[15] Furthermore, a tableau of Tutankhamun himself in battle against Asiatics existed at Karnak (fig. 45).[16] There is also a depiction of Tutankhamun charging against Asiatic foes on the painted box from his tomb.[17] On the other hand, the fact that these Asiatic scenes existed in parallel with one of Nubian campaigning (which is also the case at Karnak[18]) may, or may not, militate against their historicity. Yet Egyptian action would fit in well with the context of known Hittite activity in the crucial North Syrian border zone.[19]

Fig. 43. Syrian captives with their Egyptian guards, as shown in the tomb of Horemheb (RMO H.III.OOOO).

Fig. 44. Horemheb (shown twice) presents a delegation
of seven Asiatics and two Libyans to Tutankhamun
and Ankhesenamun to request terms in the wake of a
successful Egyptian campaign. From a relief on the west
wall of the inner courtyard of Horemheb's Saqqara
tomb (RMO H.III.QQQQ. H.III.SSSS & F1914/4.1,
Vienna 214 and Berlin 22663).

Fig. 45. Reconstruction of part of the Asiatic battle scene
from the outer part of Tutankhamun's Karnak monument.
The blocks included here were found widely dispersed,
at Medamud and Luxor as well as at Karnak.

In the north, the rump of the Mitannian state, now based at Carchemish, at length made an attempt to reassert Tushratta's authority in his former realm. In addition, there was an Egyptian attempt to regain Qadesh, perhaps following up the more southerly campaign(s) apparently depicted in Horemheb's tomb. The assault on Qadesh failed, and in retaliation the Hittites made a new attack on Amqa, which had apparently by now reverted to Egyptian control. Turning to face the Mitannians, the Hittites besieged Carchemish, which fell after a week. Tushratta escaped, but was soon murdered by a Mitannian faction, which placed one of his sons on the throne of the surviving fragments of the state, which were then ultimately swallowed up by the Assyrians.

It was as he prepared for the attack on Carchemish that Shuppiluliumash received a surprise:[20]

> When the Egyptians heard of the attack on the land of Amqa, they were afraid. Since, in addition, their lord Nipkhururiya had died, and *dakhamanzu*, who was the queen of Egypt, sent a messenger to [Shuppiluliumash]. She wrote thus to him: 'My husband died, and I have no son. But they say, you have many sons. If you would send me one of your sons, then he would become my husband. I do not want to take a servant of mine and make him my husband. I am afraid!' When [Shuppiluliumash] heard this, he called forth the Great Men for counsel (saying): 'Never before has such a thing ever happened to me!' So it came about that [Shuppiluliumash] sent Hattushaziti, the Chamberlain, into Egypt, (saying): 'Go! You must bring back to me the true word. Perhaps they are deceiving me; perhaps there is a son of their lord: you must bring back to me the true word!'

We will return to this in Chapter 5.

those who had replaced Neferneferuaten in the direction of the state on the young king's behalf. It seems clear that two figures were pivotal in this, both senior army officers: Ay and Horemheb. Their backgrounds will be considered further in Chapters 6 and 7, but at the time of their appearance under Tutankhamun, they were respectively (among other things) Overseer of horses (*imy-r ssmt*) and Generalissimo (*imy-r mš' wr*), in some cases "of the King" or "of the Lord of the Two Lands," suggesting that they were the respective heads of the chariotry and infantry arms of the Egyptian army. Horemheb was also a Noble (*iry-p't*), marking him out as a member of the ruling elite,[8] and had been since at least the year of the young king's accession.[9]

Horemheb (fig. 48) went on to be granted a vast array of additional titles,[10] perhaps most significantly King's Deputy in the Entire Land (*idnw n nsw m t3 r dr.f*, and variants) and Noble of Upper and Lower Egypt (*iry p't nw šm'w t3-mḥw*); the former is essentially unique to Horemheb,[11] while the latter becomes synonymous with "crown prince" during the Ramesside Period.[12] Militarily, he is also attested as Overseer of the Generals of the Lord of the Two Lands (*imy-r imyw-r mš' nb-t3wy*). All these titles imply a status equivalent to a king's eldest son, and the political role of regent. The latter is made explicit by the epithet "the one chosen by the king before the Two Lands to carry out the government of both river banks" and "the eyes of the king when leading the Two Lands and establishing the laws of both river banks." He was also Overseer of All Works (*imy-r k3(w)t nbt*) in some cases "of the King," and other extended forms. In contrast, Ay seems to have had a much more restricted set of titles, preferring above all God's Father (*it-ntr*).[13]

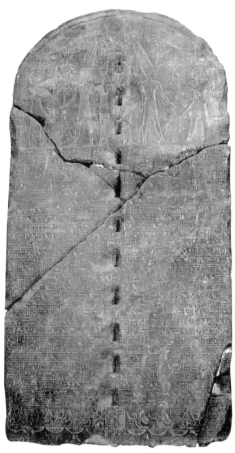

Fig. 47. Restoration Stela of Tutankhamun (Cairo CG34183).

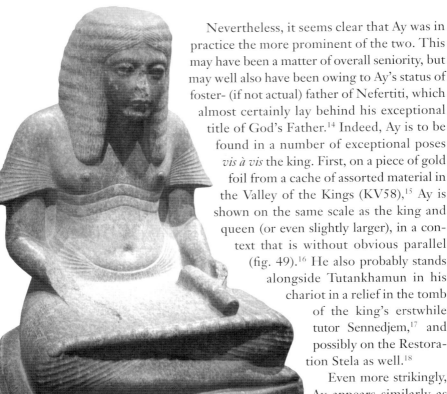

Nevertheless, it seems clear that Ay was in practice the more prominent of the two. This may have been a matter of overall seniority, but may well also have been owing to Ay's status of foster- (if not actual) father of Nefertiti, which almost certainly lay behind his exceptional title of God's Father.[14] Indeed, Ay is to be found in a number of exceptional poses *vis à vis* the king. First, on a piece of gold foil from a cache of assorted material in the Valley of the Kings (KV58),[15] Ay is shown on the same scale as the king and queen (or even slightly larger), in a context that is without obvious parallel (fig. 49).[16] He also probably stands alongside Tutankhamun in his chariot in a relief in the tomb of the king's erstwhile tutor Sennedjem,[17] and possibly on the Restoration Stela as well.[18]

Even more strikingly, Ay appears similarly as Tutankhamun's "shadow" on a number of blocks found in Pylon IX, from a temple known as the Temple of Nebkheperure Beloved of Amun Who Puts Thebes in Order (fig. 50).[19] It has been suggested that this lay on the

Fig. 48. Statue of Horemheb in scribal pose (MMA 23.10.1).

south side of the main axis of the temple, close to the Sacred Lake and Pylon VII (fig. 51), where some usurped Tutankhamun reliefs survive,[20] but it could have been elsewhere.[21] If the "Temple of Nebkheperure in Thebes" is indeed simply a later name for the same structure, the outer parts of the same building were decorated—if not entirely erected—only after Tutankhamun's death.[22] Many of its architraves and other blocks were found reused in Pylon II and seem to have come from a colonnaded court some twenty meters across;[23] they and other fragments of the building now lie in the blockyards in western part of the Karnak complex (fig. 52).

Part of the structure was built of blocks taken from Akhenaten's Karnak buildings, the raised relief carving of the new temple contrasting with the sunk relief used in the original Aten sanctuary.[24] The use of the blocks by Tutankhamun indicates that the demolition of Akhenten's East Karnak installations (maps 4 and 5) was already well under way by the latter part of Tutankhamun's reign. These blocks were ultimately widely dispersed around the Thebaid, turning up not only in Pylon II, but also in the area of the Luxor temple and at Medamud.[25]

The motifs included in the decoration of the temple covered the standard repertoire of Eighteenth Dynasty temples—offering scenes, festival and offering lists, bark processions, and the like. However, they also included a tableau of a chariot battle against the Asiatics in which Tutankhamun was the central figure (fig. 45), together with its

Fig. 49. Fragment of gold foil showing Tutankhamun smiting an enemy while Ay and Ankhesenamun raise their hands in praise. From KV58 (Cairo JE57438).

Fig. 50. Tutankhamun followed by the carefully erased figure of an official—certainly Ay—on a block recovered from the core of the west tower of Pylon IX at Karnak.

aftermath,[26] and another commemorating a Nubian campaign.[27] The historicity of this pairing of scenes on either side of the court is questionable, but may be linked with presentation of captives scenes in the Saqqara tomb of Horemheb,[28] and possibly the representation of a *durbar* in the tomb of the Nubian viceroy Huy (fig. 55).[29]

Besides this temple, Tutankhamun was responsible for laying out the sphinx avenue that led from the southern gateway of the Amun complex—at Tutankhamun's accession the incomplete Pylon X of Amenhotep III—to the nearby temple of Mut (fig. 53 and map 4).[30] The actual sphinxes were, however, secondhand, some having been made to represent Akhenaten and some to represent Nefertiti, and presumably they once formed part of the east Karnak Aten complex. Now they were decapitated, given new rams' heads, and further adorned with a small figure of Tutankhamun.[31] It seems that the installation of the sphinxes was under way at Tutankhamun's death and continued later, as the southern part of the avenue was completed in the name of Ay. All cartouches were later usurped by Horemheb. Although Horemheb actually finished and decorated Pylon X, it is not impossible that some work was carried out there by Tutankhamun in connection with the construction of the sphinx avenue.

In addition to the new building work at Karnak, a further major project was the replacement or repair of the images of Amun that had been the target of Akhenaten's spite all over Egypt. The sheer quantity was such

Fig. 51. Aerial view of the central part of the Karnak Temple, looking west. Suggestions for possible locations of the Tutankhamun/Ay temple have included the area just north-west of the Sacred Lake and on the south side of what is now the courtyard between Pylons I and II (see map 5). However, nothing has yet been located on the ground, only the blocks recovered from pylon fill; some of these are stored in the block field at top left.

Fig. 52. Architrave from the Temple of Nebkheperure at Thebes, discovered in the core of Horemheb's Pylon II: note the unmutilated state of the inscriptions (cf. p. 119, below).

that only a proportion of two-dimensional depictions had been recarved by the end of Tutankhamun's reign. The rest had to await later rulers' ministrations, in particular by Horemheb, Sethy I, and Rameses II—who in many cases also claimed credit for, or even reworked, Tutankhamun's restorations.[32] There were also new additions to existing work, one of the most notable being the insertion of a small figure of Tutankhamun behind each of two figures of Amenhotep III in a relief on the rear face of Pylon III at Karnak (fig. 54).[33] This was presumably an attempt to associate Tutankhamun formally with his most recent "acceptable" ancestor—both his parents now clearly not being so—a link that is reinforced in a number of important contexts.

Most prominent is Tutankhamun's completion of Amenhotep III's entrance colonnade at the Luxor Temple (fig. 55).[34] At the old king's death, decoration had only just begun, but what had been done was attacked by Akhenaten and now needed restoration.[35] The key part of Tutankhamun's work was, however, the completion and adornment of the walls of the colonnade with an extensive depiction of the Opet festival, one of the key events of the Theban year. It would appear that the laying out of the decorative scheme was entirely carried out as a single project under Tutankhamun, but the last stages of the actual carving dragged on into the reign of Sethy I.[36]

Fig. 53. Tutankhamun's sphinx avenue at Karnak, leading from Pylon X toward the Mut temple.

Fig. 54. One of the two images of Tutankhamun added behind Amenhotep III on the rear of Pylon III at Karnak. They were subsequently erased and replaced by carvings of offering tables but are still visible as ghostly outlines.

It is probable that the king spent some time as a resident at Malqata, as a ring bezel from there bears the king's prenomen, and a document seal bears the name of Queen Ankhesenamun; a further bezel naming simply "Ankhesenpaaten" might date to the first phase of her husband's reign, or that of Akhenaten, whose name also appears on bezels from Malqata. A door-jamb that was later usurped by Horemheb might have originally belonged to Tutankhamun.[37]

Amenhotep III's monuments also received attention in faraway Soleb in Nubia.[38] One[39] of a pair of granite lions[40] that had been commissioned for the temple under its founder was finished[41] and dedicated to "his father" by Tutankhamun, perhaps hereby once again tying himself to his grandfather, rather than his actual father.[42] This skipping of a generation is also seen on a wooden astronomical instrument, on which Tutankhamun apparently calls Thutmose IV "father of his father."[43]

Even further south, Tutankhamun (re)constructed Temple A at Kawa, "setting up what had been in ruins."[44] Here, there are reasons for believing that Tutankhamun was deified in the temple as a form of Amun-Re, after the manner of a number of New Kingdom monarchs in Nubia.[45] In Lower Nubia, at Faras, a temple was built by Tutankhamun's viceroy

Fig. 55. Luxor Temple, with the Great Colonnade, decorated by Tutankhamun, in the center.

of Nubia, Huy.[46] The latter's tomb survives on Qurnet Murai at Thebes West (TT40), and includes a number of scenes of the presentation of foreign tribute to the king (fig. 56),[47] reminiscent on a smaller scale of Akhenaten's great *durbar* reliefs.[48]

A number of Huy's immediate subordinates are named in TT40, one of them being the Fortress Commander of Faras, Penniut. This man advanced before the end of Tutankhamun's reign to being Deputy of Wawat (Lower Nubia), as is known from a stela from Kurkur Oasis, some sixty kilometers southwest of Aswan.[49] This source is also useful for elucidating the border control regime of the Nubian province at this time.

The other site with physical evidence for state building work under Tutankhamun is Memphis, a city whose status seems to increase markedly in his reign; indeed, it seems to have been from this city that the decree published on the Restoration Stela was issued.[50] For a number of reasons, including the burial of a considerable number of officials in the area (see below), it seems that with the move of the royal residence from Amarna, the old northern capital became much more of an equal partner with

Thebes, heralding the major expansion of the Ptah temple there onto virgin land early in the Nineteenth Dynasty.

As far as Tutankhamun is concerned, the existence of a House of Nebkheperure at Memphis is attested by a stela (of its treasurer, May) carved into the wall of the sanctuary of Sekhmet that had been set up during the Eighteenth Dynasty in the Old Kingdom mortuary temple of Sahure at Abu Sir.[51] At Memphis itself, fragments from Tutankhamun's building works may include a lintel found built into the Twenty-second Dynasty tomb-chamber of the high priest Shoshenq D (fig. 57),[52] and possibly a further lintel bought on the antiquities market.[53] Of Tutankhamun's time also are a private votive stela depicting the king before Ptah,[54] together with a tourist graffito by a certain Tjay in the Step Pyramid enclosure at Saqqara.[55]

Saqqara also saw the burial of an Apis bull, the third such interment known, the first having been made by Tutankhamun's short-lived uncle, Thutmose B, while high priest at Memphis.[56] Work in the area of Heliopolis is suggested by the presence of fragments reused in the construction of

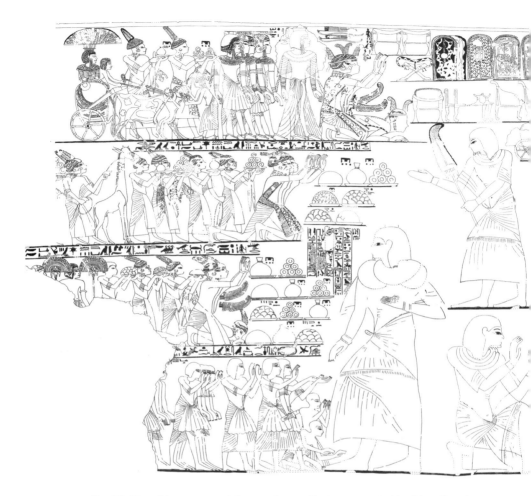

Fig. 56. Tutankhamun receiving southern tribute, presented by Huy, the viceroy of Nubia, in TT40. One of the Nubian chieftains at the front of the top-left

the tomb of a Mnevis bull under Rameses II, which had been usurped by Horemheb from Tutankhamun.[57]

Finally for the Memphite region, Tutankhamun added a doorway[58] to a large brick structure of uncertain purpose (long misnamed the "Resthouse of Tutankhamun") lying southeast of Khaefre's valley temple at Giza. A private stela showing a now-anonymous official paying his respects to the king and queen was also found nearby, in front of the Sphinx Temple.[59]

In contrast to these items from the traditional centers, only one ring bezel and a mold apparently attest to activity by Tutankh*amun* at Amarna.[60]

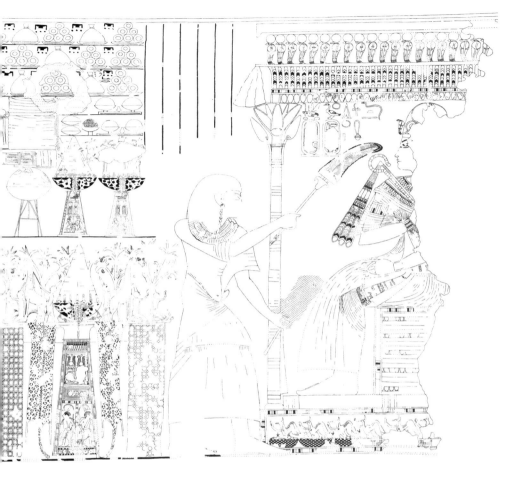

register is Heqanefer, also known from his tomb at Toshka where, interestingly, he is shown as if Egyptian.

Nevertheless, as there is material that points to continued official activity at Amarna until as late as the reign of Horemheb,[61] there is likely to have been a continued, if diminishing, administrative presence there throughout Tutankhamun's later reign.

The removal of the court from Amarna also terminated that city's role as a state necropolis: TA27 and TA28 were never finished, while there is no firm evidence for any of the nobles' tombs having been used for a burial. This left the royal interments, and it would seem likely that these were removed to Thebes soon after Tutankhamun's change of name,[62] although the only

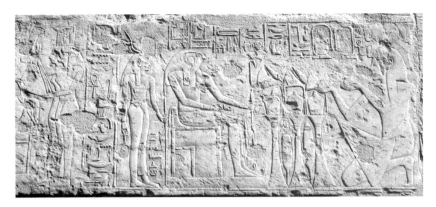

Fig. 57. Right-hand end of a lintel of Tutankhamun, usurped by Horemheb, and reused in the Twenty-second Dynasty tomb of Shoshenq D at Memphis (Cairo JE88131).

identifiable example of such a reburial is KV55.[63] It had clearly been interfered with and material was removed at a later date, but the presence in the deposit of "magic bricks" of Akhenaten and what seems to be the mummy of Smenkhkare would suggest that the bodies of at least these two kings were originally moved from the Amarna Royal Wadi to KV55. The additional presence of the shrine of Queen Tiye may indicate that the queen's mummy may also have been brought along, although the shrine might rather have been used to provide a shelter for the two kings' coffins, her mummy being moved directly to the tomb of Amenhotep III.

However, as noted above, the deposit was no longer in its original form when excavated, with the one remaining body left nameless, and Akhenaten's images removed from the shrine. It would thus seem that when the tomb was reentered, Akhenaten's mummy was removed (presumably for destruction),[64] the body of Smenkhkare stripped of its identity, and a beginning made of removing the shrine from the tomb, a move frustrated by the narrowness of the opening made in the doorway.[65] As for the date of this desecration, this has often been placed in Ramesside times,[66] but it now seems clear that the site of KV55 was entirely covered as a result of a flash flood not long after the final closure of Tutankhamun's tomb.[67]

Since it is unlikely that Tutankhamun would have authorized such treatment of his father and uncle's reburials, the desecration can on this basis only have occurred under Ay (or conceivably during the very first years of the reign of Horemheb) since a geological analysis suggests only a short interval between the last sealing of KV55 and the flood.[68]

Fig. 58. Statues of Amun and Amunet at Karnak, erected during the reigns of Tutankhamun and Ay respectively.

Fig. 59. Statue of Amun and Mut, carved with the features of Tutankhamun (destroyed) and Ankhesenamun as mature individuals. From Luxor Temple cache (Luxor Museum).

The fate of the other mummies in TA26 remains wholly obscure,[69] but it would seem not unlikely that a deposit akin to KV55 was prepared for them. If it was in the Valley of the Kings, it could possibly be a potential tomb that has been located by remote sensing close to Tutankhamun's.[70] Such a cache could also have been a convenient place to dispose of the mummy of Neferneferuaten, but this is of course pure speculation.

Above and beyond Tutankhamun's building activity was the manufacture of divine figures, an activity highlighted in the Restoration Stela and a necessary remedy for Akhenaten's iconoclasm, particularly against Amun. Thus a very considerable number of three-dimensional representations of members of the Theban triad survive, from both Karnak and Luxor, bearing the features of Tutankhamun.[71] Nearly all were later usurped by Horemheb,[72] but all are recognizable by their distinctive facial appearance (e.g., figs. 58–61).

The "Tutankhamunesque" style is also to be seen in two dimensions, and while retaining some of the elegance of the mature Amarna art style, it reverts to the pre-Amarna proportions used in laying out human images.[73] A good demonstration of this is seen when comparing two figures found together in the tomb of Tutankhamun, showing a king on the back of a black leopard. One was originally made for Neferneferuaten (fig. 29)[74] and clearly fits into the Amarna canon; on the other hand its companion, made for Tutankhamun,[75] was made in accordance with orthodox proportions.[76] On the other hand, anomalies exist, and there was clearly a protracted re-education process for those who had been trained in the Amarna school to move into what was once again the prescribed way of depicting a human being, but without ever fully returning to pre-Amarna models.[77]

Both Ay and Horemheb apparently stood outside the normal hierarchy of the Egyptian state, the exceptional status of the latter being potentially indicated by a block from the tomb of the high priest of Ptah Ptahemhat-Ty, which shows the priest's funeral procession headed by an unnamed Generalissimo who is usually identified as Horemheb (fig. 62).[78] He is there shown as clearly senior to the two viziers, normally the highest in the land after the king, not to mention the rest of the mourners, who include a Royal Steward, a Royal Treasurer, the Overseer of the Law Court, a general, a chamberlain, the Overseer of the Treasury, and the Heliopolitan high priest.

The vizierate, originally a unitary office, had been by the late Eighteenth Dynasty split between Upper and Lower Egypt. The principal Upper Egyptian holder of the office during Tutankhamun's reign was Usermontju, named on a fragment of statue which included a cartouche that had almost certainly once been that of Tutankhamun.[79] He is later shown in the tombs of two of his apparent descendants,[80] and was buried somewhere in the Theban necropolis.[81] Another vizier—it is unclear whether of the north or the south—was Pentju, known only from a wine-jar docket found in the tomb of Tutankhamun. It has been suggested that he was none other than the former owner of tomb TA5 at Amarna, but this cannot be proven.[82]

A key question concerning the vizierate is whether Ay ever held that title. Given his unique ascendancy, one would not necessarily

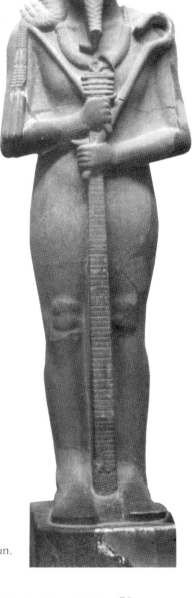

Fig. 60. Khonsu depicted with the face of Tutankhamun. From Karnak, temple of Khonsu (Cairo CG38488).

expect him to hold such a title, but a gold foil fragment from KV58, found alongside that shown in fig. 49, and all but certainly referring to Ay, bears the title Priest of Maat, generally associated with viziers, together with an epithet that seems to read "vizier, doer of Maat" (*t3ty iri m3ʿt*).[83] However, the latter is not a formulation used by a regular vizier, and thus may not necessarily denote Ay as a holder of either formal vizierate.[84] On the other hand it is possible that he may have used the title of vizier in some kind of extraordinary manner, rather than holding one or more of the regional posts.

Few other members of the civil administration are known, but Maya, the Overseer of the Treasury and Overseer of Works in the Place of Eternity, was clearly a person of importance[85] and would later donate two fine funerary figures to Tutankhamun's funerary outfit.[86] He lived on into the reign of Horemheb.[87] A fragment of stela records a decree on Year 8, IV *prt*, day 22, commanding Maya to "tax the whole land and institute divine offerings [for] all the [gods] of the land of Egypt . . ."—presumably to facilitate the rededication of some of the now restored temples.[88]

It is possible that Maya may be same man as the May who had a tomb (TA14) at Amarna[89] and shared many of his titles—but not, crucially, the Treasury post. On the other hand, a statue of a May[90] had this office added secondarily to its list of titles, which might support the equation of the two men. It is also possible that a royal scribe Maya, attested in Year 34 of Amenhotep III, at Malqata,[91] could be the same individual.

Other known officials include an Overseer of the Cattle of Amun, Pay, known from his tomb at Saqqara,[92] and a Royal Scribe named Merymery, attested by a stela recording a land transaction;[93] while from the provinces we also know of a mayor of Thinis, near Abydos, named Seba.[94] Further individuals known to have been active late in the Eighteenth Dynasty doubtless had careers that included at least parts of Tutankhamun's reign, but cannot be pinned down with certainty.

In Nubia, the viceroyalty was held by Amenhotep-Huy, well known from his tomb-chapel on Qurnet Murai at Thebes (TT40), successor to one Thutmose, and possibly a former subordinate of Merymose who had been viceroy under Amenhotep III.[95] A number of Huy's officials are also known, including the governor of Kawa, Panakht,[96] and one of the local chieftains, Heqanefer, who is known both from his own tomb at Toshka East (number I) and from his depiction in Huy's tomb (fig. 56).[97]

Little is known of the holders of the principal high priesthoods of the reign. At Karnak, we are ignorant of the name of the incumbent,[98] likewise at Heliopolis; at Memphis the high priest was Ptahemhat-Ty, whose Saqqara

Fig. 61. Triad, with Tutankhamun between Amun and Mut. From Karnak (Cairo CG42097).

Fig. 62. Block from the tomb of Ptahemhat-Ty at Saqqara, showing the head of his funeral procession. The leading figure is not named, but his title and precedence over the two viziers seen further back makes it all but certain that he is either Horemheb or Nakhtmin B, depending on the reign in which the piece was produced (Berlin 12411).

funeral procession has been noted above.[99] Also at Saqqara is the tomb of the high priest of the Aten, Meryneith, whose career had begun in the early reign of Akhenaten. At that period he changed his name to Meryre, and then reverted to his original name under Tutankhamun.[100]

This tomb formed part of a group that included some important sepulchers of Tutankhamun's reign, in particular those of Horemheb and the treasurer Maya (fig. 63).[101] Meryneith's tomb indicates that the use of this particular area extends back at least into the earlier part of Akhenaten's reign, with its use for high-status primary interments stretching on into the Nineteenth Dynasty.[102] As well as this group of tombs, in the southern part of the cemetery, the latter part of the Eighteenth Dynasty also sees the appearance of tombs further north at Saqqara, around the pyramid of Teti[103] and in the escarpment overlooking Memphis.[104] Tombs also appear much further south at Dahshur.[105] This contrasts strongly with the pre-Amarna New Kingdom situation when significant tombs in the Memphite necropolis are rare.

There have been suggestions that this could be a result of a shift in the post-Amarna funerary ideology,[106] but as the renewed construction of high status tombs at Saqqara began back at the end of the reign of Amenhotep III,[107] it is rather unlikely to have been a primary reason. Rather, it may simply be a social phenomenon, whereby it was now no longer regarded as *de rigeur* to return to Thebes in death, no matter where one actually lived and worked. This might have gained an additional impetus from the explicit rejection of Thebes by Akhenaten in favor of Amarna, with the fashion continuing into the new climate of Tutankhamun's reign.

Fig. 63. The southern New Kingdom necropolis at Saqqara. From the left: the tombs of Pay and Raia, Horemheb, Tia and Tjia, and Maya; on the far right, Meryneith/re. In the distance is the Fifth Dynasty pyramid of Unas.

Running parallel with the civil administration was that of the army. As compared with earlier periods, New Kingdom Egypt had a far more extensive and formally organized set of military forces and command hierarchy.[108] Soldiers are prominent at Amarna, frequently being seen in tomb scenes clearing the way for the royal family during their progress to the Central City (fig. 9), and it is instructive that the two leading men of the state after the demise of Neferneferuaten were military men.[109]

While Ay seems to have taken a primarily civil role under Tutankhamun—his military title is used only occasionally—Horemheb continues to make prominent his role as a senior army officer, including in his tomb scenes explicit reference to military activity.[110] However, little is known of other individuals in the army hierarchy; the only exception is the General Nakhtmin (B) who dedicated five fine shabtis to Tutankhamun's burial.[111] There is evidence that he may have been Ay's son,[112] demonstrating the important family ramifications of the period.

Beyond the aforementioned stela recording the tax decree of Year 8, very little is known as to precise events during the second half of Tutankhamun's reign. One assumes that much of the time was taken up with the implementation of the measures set out in the Restoration Stela—which indeed seems to be what the Year 8 stela is dealing with. However, one activity during this period must have been the preparation of a tomb for the king.

As noted above, it seems that a tomb was begun for Tutankhaten at Amarna; on the court's removal from that city a new tomb will have been needed in the ancestral cemetery at Thebes-West. There may have been a delay in the beginning of work there, especially if the Workmen's Village at Amarna was indeed populated by personnel from the Theban workmen's community of Deir el-Medina,[113] and perhaps there was also an issue as to where the tomb should be located. Tutankhamun's grandfather, Amenhotep III, had his sepulcher in the hitherto virgin western branch of the Valley of the Kings (WV22), and it seems likely that Amenhotep IV had begun a tomb (WV25) at the far end of this side valley before the move to Amarna.[114] It is not impossible that Tutankhamun's officials contemplated the continuation of this, but its attenuated state suggests that it was probably not worked upon further.

The tomb in the main Valley of the Kings (KV57) ultimately used by Horemheb could have been begun for Tutankhamun, but the broad consensus has been that the king's intended burial place was WV23, only a short distance from WV25 (figs. 64 and 65). This was eventually taken over for

Ay as king, and it has been suggested that Tutankhamun was actually buried there, but was subsequently moved to make way for Ay.[115] However, it is more generally assumed that the tomb was incomplete at Tutankhamun's death and alternative arrangements were consequently made.

The other element of Tutankhamun's funerary installation, his memorial temple, is likely also to have been in an unfinished state. Indeed, no definite trace of the building has ever come to light, but it is highly unlikely that nothing was even begun. A potential clue to its location lies in the fact that both Amenhotep III and Tutankhamun's own successor founded their memorial temples just north of what is now Medinet Habu: just as the presence of the burials of these two kings in the West Valley suggests Tutankhamun's intended interment there, their temples' location may hint at where Tutankhamun's lost temple may have lain.

Of course, the possibility that Tutankhamun's unfinished sanctuary was taken over by Ay is attractive, but the excavation of the temple intended for Ay revealed only Ay's own foundation deposits[116] and nothing of Tutankhamun, apart from a pair of statues, whose style has suggested that they might have been made for him.[117] On the other hand, the remains of two anonymous temples exist between the temples of Amenhotep III and Ay. These are known as the North Temple and the South Temple, due to their positions with respect to the memorial temples for Amenhotep III's distinguished official, Amenhotep-son-of-Hapu, and Thutmose II (figs. 66 and 67).[118] That the North and South Temples should date to the later Eighteenth Dynasty is suggested by the similarities between their plans and that of Amenhotep-son-of-Hapu's sanctuary, while the fact that Rameses IV laid out a temple over part of the site of the North Temple[119] shows that the latter had been demolished by the early Twentieth Dynasty. Given Tutankhamun's apparent wish to be associated with Amenhotep III, the North Temple might be the more attractive candidate, but as absolutely no inscribed material has been found at either site, the South Temple certainly cannot be ruled out.[120]

The unfinished nature of the funerary monuments of Tutankhamun attests to the unexpectedness of his death, as well as the limited time available for their preparation after the move away from Amarna. The tomb in which he was actually buried (KV62: fig. 65) is almost universally agreed to be a modestly extended private tomb.[121] Royally favored private individuals had been buried in the Valley of the Kings since at least the middle of the Eighteenth Dynasty, placing their burial chambers here rather than the usual location in or close to their tomb-chapels on the other side of the Theban

Fig. 64. The end of the West Valley of the Kings, showing locations of tombs WV23 (far right) and WV25 (center).

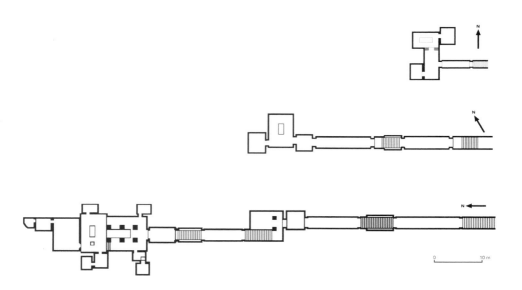

Fig. 65. Plans of the tombs of Tutankhamun (KV62), Ay (KV23) and Horemheb (KV57).

cliffs.[122] The best-preserved example of such an interment is that of Yuya and Tjuiu in KV46,[123] whose plan is very similar to the probable original layout of KV62, the tomb in which Tutankhamun was laid to rest.

While it is usually assumed that such a tomb was used as a direct consequence of the unfinished state of the proper tomb, it is worth pointing out that a few decades later, when faced with a similar situation, those responsible for Rameses I's burial did something very different. Rather than find a new tomb, the king's proper tomb (KV16) had a small burial chamber added just beyond the point reached by the tomb cutters at the king's death. The same could certainly have been done for Tutankhamun in (probably) WV23. So why was it not?

The reason may be tied up with the location nearby of KV55. This tomb lies close to KV62 at about the same level in the center of the valley,[124] and it is possible that the availability of a private tomb nearby led to a decision to bury Tutankhamun close to his relations. Whatever the motivation, the tomb was enlarged, with a sunken burial crypt created just large enough to contain the nest of shrines that had sheltered the royal sarcophagus since the reign of Amenhotep II.[125] This enlargement would have taken place during the period between the king's death and his burial—a period that traditionally (although apparently seldom in practice[126]) lasted seventy days. In addition, provision seems to have been made for burying the material left over at the end of the embalming process, in a shaft-tomb (KV63) a short distance from KV62.[127]

The only part of the actual tomb to be decorated was the burial chamber, and with its small size came the need to heavily abbreviate the decorative scheme of the tomb (fig. 68). The figures of the king and deities, which would normally have adorned the pillars of the burial hall and the antechambers, were placed on the long walls. The Book of Amduat that had covered the walls of earlier burial halls was stripped down to a few vignettes from the first hour (only) on the wall at the head of the body. The decoration was completed, on the wall at the foot of the sarcophagus, by a scene of the mummy dragged to the tomb—a unique representation for a royal burial chamber, but a staple of private tomb-chapels—together with a scene of the Opening of the Mouth ceremony.

The cause of the death of the king, in his tenth regnal year, at an age of around eighteen, has been a matter for debate ever since the body was first examined. The first examination of the body by Douglas Derry during and after the unwrapping was unable to identify any cause of death.[128] An x-ray taken in 1968 of the king's head led, however, to

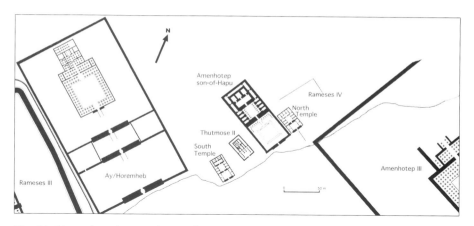

Fig. 66. Map of Medinet Habu north.

Fig. 67. View of Medinet Habu area from the west, showing the locations of the following memorial temples: A – Amenhotep III; B – Rameses IV; C – North Temple; D – Amenhotep son of Hapu; E – Thutmose II; F – South Temple; G – Ay/Horemheb; H – Rameses III.

some researchers detecting traces of a possible blow at the base of his skull, leading to a rash of theories that Tutankhamun had been murdered, some spun out into lurid detail, with Ay often confidently stated to be the murderer.[129]

Then a CAT scan in 2005 concluded there was nothing wrong with the king's head, and the alleged injury was simply an artifact of a misaligned x-ray plate. However, a fracture across the top of the left femur was considered by a number of investigators to be a possible cause—a compound fracture could easily become infected, with potentially rapid mortality in the absence of modern drugs. On the other hand, this conclusion has not been universally accepted, and for the time being one can only regard the cause of death as remaining unproven.[130]

Regardless of the cause of his death, Tutankhamun's sudden demise must have thrown plans for the royal burial into confusion. On the other hand, the actual interment seems not to have lacked any items of equipment; indeed, comparison of Tutankhamun's equipment with the remains of equivalent items found in other royal tombs indicates it was in some ways richer than earlier outfits, in that Tutankhamun had gilded versions of items that were usually simply black-varnished.[131]

We have already noted that a considerable number of items made for the burial of Neferneferuaten—not to mention a coffin of Smenkhkare, and possibly pieces made for Amenhotep IV—were adapted for Tutankhamun's burial. This has not infrequently been used as an argument for the hurried nature of the burial, with the need to appropriate material to make up numbers. However, it is hardly credible that such valuable items could have been left gathering dust for last-minute appropriation. Far more likely is that, as soon as it became clear that items would not be required for their original owner, they were reworked to become the first elements of the new ruler's burial outfit. Thus, rather than being a mark of last-minute panic, the "Neferneferuaten inheritance" probably meant that Tutankhamun was the possessor of an exceptionally complete burial outfit—contrasting with his incomplete actual tomb.

Estimating the time line for the preparation of Tutankhamun's tomb depends on being able to estimate the relative dates of his death and burial. The only criterion for the latter seems to be the floral remains from the tomb which, if they were used fresh, place the funeral in March/April.[132] For the timing of his death, the evidence comes from the unexpected source already mentioned at the end of the previous chapter, which will now be considered in more detail.

5 THE ZANANZASH AFFAIR

The key document for the death of Tutankhamun is the account quoted at the end of Chapter 3. Over the years there has been considerable debate as to the identity of "Nipkhururiya," and the *dakhamanzu* who wrote so dramatically to Shuppiluliumash as he prepared to besiege Carchemish.[1] It has long been recognized that *dakhamanzu* is simply an Akkadian transcription of the Egyptian *t3 ḥmt-nsw*, "the king's wife": but which one? The majority view has generally been that she was Ankhesenamun, the widow of Tutankhamun, not only on circumstantial grounds, but also because it is his prenomen that is properly transcribed into Akkadian as Nipkhururiya, as quoted in the Hittite text: for it to be anyone else, an error on the part of the ancient scribe must be presumed.[2] Nevertheless, it has been suggested that she might have been Nefertiti or Meryetaten on the death of Akhenaten, or even Meryetaten on the death of Smenkhkare, and that the Hittite scribe indeed made a slip in quoting the king's name. However, emendation should always be a last resort; and in any case, on the reconstruction already put forward in this book, Nefertiti was a king by the time Akhenaten died, with a son to place on the throne,[3] while Smenkhkare had died some time before Akhenaten. Kiya has also been proposed, but all the evidence argues for her disgrace well before Akhenaten's death.[4] Thus the identification of *dakhamanzu* with Ankhesenamun remains by far the most credible option.

The sending of the first letter by the queen, and hence the death of Tutankhamun, can be dated approximately by its having taken place prior to the siege of Carchemish, where operations and subsequent arrangements would have had to be completed before the onset of the Anatolian winter brought the campaigning season to a close. On this basis, Tutankhamun would have died at the end of the summer or in the early autumn,[5] giving a gap of some six months between his death and his burial in March/April of the following year[6]—double the normal period. Some of this might have been legitimately taken up with additional works necessitated by the incomplete state of the king's burial arrangements, but one is strongly tempted to suspect that unfolding events lay behind this excessive delay.

It seems fairly clear that carrying out the funeral was a key act in the formal transmission of goods and offices between the generations, even more so when no blood descendant existed.[7] Thus, in normal circumstances one would have expected Tutankhamun's burial to take place as soon as practicable, to allow the situation to be regularized. The fact that the seals used to close Tutankhamun's tomb bore his own name rather than that of his successor[8] suggests that the formal close of a king's reign may have been at his burial, with the beginning of the new one marked by the new king carrying out the burial. That this in practice may have led to a short period of (nominally) both a living and a dead king is shown by the depiction of Tutankhamun's successor, as king, on the burial chamber wall,[9] and a seal impression of the new king that was dropped in the tomb's antechamber.[10]

Where that left his successor between the day of death and the day of the funeral is somewhat unclear, especially as the theory of the continuity of kingship would imply a seamless transition between the reigns.[11] This concept is evident in the autobiography of Ineni in TT81 where "[Thutmose II] went forth to heaven, having mingled with the gods, and his son stood in his place as king of the Two Lands, having become ruler upon the throne of the one who begat him."[12] On the other hand, the Palermo Stone may imply an interregnum of forty-five days between the reigns of Hor-Aha and Djer, which could be apposite here.[13]

One suspects that in the vast majority of cases, where there was an undisputed eldest son, there was no real problem: he had probably already been formally nominated as crown prince,[14] and will simply have assumed an untrammeled royal dignity on his father's death, the funeral and subsequent coronation being a matter of routine. However, where there was no such individual, matters would have been more problematic—as now on Tutankhamun's death. Was there an interregnum—and if so, who would have been in charge during that period?

Looking at the Hittite data, it would appear that there was indeed an interregnum, and that authority rested with the dowager queen—as most probably would also have been the case had Tutankhamun left a child who was still a minor.[15] When Shuppiluliumash's envoy Hattushaziti returned from Egypt in the spring, he brought with him Hani, an Egyptian emissary, and a letter from the queen:

> Why did you speak in this way, 'they deceive me'? If I had a son, would I have written about the shame of myself and of my land to another land? You did not trust me, and even spoke to me in that way! He who was my husband has died. I have no son. I do not want to take a servant of mine and make him my husband. I have not written to any other land, I wrote to you! They say you have many sons: give me one of your sons; to me he will be husband, but in the land of Egypt he will be king!

The queen's letter was backed up by Hani when Shuppiluliumash cross-examined him, pointing out that there had been recent hostilities between the two powers, in particular the attack on Qadesh and the Hittite reprisal against Amqa. Shuppiluliumash wondered whether the letter was some kind of trick to deliver a Hittite prince into Egyptian hands and then to turn him into a hostage.

Hani responded in much the same way as the queen had done in her letter:

> My lord, this [is] the shame of our land: if there was any [prince], would we come to another land? Would we request a lord for ourselves? Nipkhururiya, who was our lord, has died. A son of his does not exist. The wife of our lord is childless. We desire a son of our lord in the land of Egypt for kingship. For the woman, our lady, we desire him as her husband. Further, we did not go to any other land, we came only here! Our lord, give us a son of yours!

Had anyone been installed as king, even in a caretaker role, one can hardly expect this not to have been noticed by the Hittite ambassador—or that Hani would have perjured himself before the Hittite king. On the basis of this, Shuppiluliumash thus resolved to send a son: 'Formerly Hattusas and Egypt were at peace with each other. Now this, too, has occurred between us. Therefore, the land of Hatti [and] the land of Egypt will be in eternal friendship with each other!'

The key question in all this is how far the call for a Hittite prince was an agreed position by the Egyptian court, or how far it was an initiative by a faction centering on Ankhesenamun. Was the delay in Tutankhamun's burial planned in order to accommodate the delays at the Hittite end, or was the burial being held up on other pretexts: to prevent an Egyptian candidate from carrying out the funeral, and give time for the Hittite candidate to arrive belatedly from Anatolia?

The view taken on this impacts upon how one should interpret what happened next. Although the immediately following parts of the Deeds of Shuppiluliumash are too broken to provide any useful information, we then read, in a broken, but basically comprehensible passage:[16]

> And they [. . .] one to another [. . .] they brought this tablet, and they spoke in this way: ['. . .] killed [Zananzash,'] and they brought word, 'Zananzash [died?' When] my father heard of the murder of Zananzash, [he] began to weep for Zananzash. He spoke [. . .] to the gods in this way, 'Oh, gods! I did [nothing] evil, [but] the men of Egypt did [that to me] and they [attacked] the borders of my land!'

It is by no means certain that Zananzash was indeed the prince sent by Shuppiluliumash in response to the Egyptian queen's request, but from the context this seems difficult to doubt. As to how or where the death had occurred there is no indication: it could have been en route, or it could have been in Egypt itself. Zananzash could have been killed by violence, or he could have succumbed to natural causes—a plague was current in the very Egyptian Syrian territories that Zananzash would have had to cross at this very time.[17]

Nevertheless, there would almost certainly have been some opposition within the Egyptian court to the idea of handing the throne to a foreigner, and some attempt at his assassination would have been a not unexpected outcome of the adventure. This was certainly the formal Hittite view, as summarized in the Second Plague Prayer of Murshilish II:

> [Shuppiluliumash . . .] attacked Amqa, Egyptian territory . . . .
> When the Egyptians became frightened, they asked outright for one of his sons to (take over) the kingship, but when [Shuppiluliumash] gave them one of his sons, they killed him as they led him there.

Fig. 69. Ay and Tey as shown in their tomb-chapel at Amarna (TA25).

other she was Nurse who Reared the Divine Lady (*mn't 3t mḥdt nṯrt*), and more explicitly Nurse of the King's Great Wife Neferneferuaten-Nefertiti (*mn't n ḥmt-nsw-wrt Nfr-nfrw-Itn Nfrt-iy-ti*, as on fig. 69). Clearly she cannot thus have been Nefertiti's mother, but this certainly does not rule out Ay having been Nefertiti's father: given the high maternal mortality rates in ancient Egypt, it is quite possible that this title should be interpreted as marking out Tey as Nefertiti's stepmother.[19]

Unfortunately, there is no definitive evidence to prove either hypothesis regarding Ay's affiliations, and it has also been argued strongly that the title God's Father simply denotes a distinguished individual who was signally honoured by the king. Tey might simply have been the queen's tutor—the title can mean both wet nurse and tutor—and this might have contributed to her husband's status.[20] On the other hand, in his decoration of the Temple of Nebkheperure in Thebes, Ay later calls Tutankhamun "his son."[21] This has generally been dismissed as rhetoric,[22] but if Ay were indeed Nefertiti's father and if, as has been argued above, Nefertiti were Tutankhamun's mother, Ay would have been Tutankhamun's actual grandfather, and quite entitled to refer to him as his (grand)son. Certainly such a reconstruction amply explains both Ay's exceptional position vis à vis Tutankhamun—and possibly his maintenance of his God's Father title, which was perhaps then reinterpreted as God's (Grand)father—and why he would have been by far the most credible Egyptian candidate after Tutankhamun's untimely death.

It would also mean that the Sister of the King's Great Wife who appears in a number of Amarna tomb-chapels[23] would also be Ay's daughter, and presumably (as apparently she is much younger than Nefertiti) a child of Tey. Her name has proven problematic, because while the first element "Mut" is clear, the second sign is less so, and could be 𓆼, *nḏm*, or 𓆽, *bnr*.[24] Both mean "sweet," but the reading of the name as Mutnodjmet on one hand, or Mutbenret on the other hand is potentially significant, as Horemheb was to marry a Mutnodjmet. We will return to this issue in the next chapter, but it would appear that the sign is sufficiently ambiguous that

Fig. 70. Fragmentary statue of Nakhtmin B and his wife. From Sheikh Abd el-Qurna (Cairo CG779).

any argument based solely on the name's *not* reading "Mutnodjmet" cannot be regarded as definitive.[25]

As for sons, the Generalissimo Nakhtmin (B) who, as a General, had donated shabtis to the burial of Tutankhamun, seems to have been a son of Ay. The evidence comes in the form of a badly broken statue that depicted Nakhtmin and his wife (fig. 70);[26] on its rear Nakhtmin's titles have been mutilated, but are just readable, giving the sequence: Royal Scribe, Generalissimo, and King's Son [. . .] before the remainder is broken away. Some have wished to restore "of Kush," making Nakhtmin a Nubian viceroy,[27] but this has been rejected by others on the grounds that no real place exists for him among the viceroys of the late Eighteenth Dynasty.[28] The only other restoration option at this period is "King's Son of his Body," i.e., an actual child of a king. As Nakhtmin's donation to the burial of Tutankhamun lacked such a title, it follows that he became a King's Son only subsequently, and the only viable time is during the reign of Ay, as the damage to the statue is almost certainly a result of the anti-Ay campaign that was undertaken during Horemheb's reign.[29]

On what seems to be a slightly earlier companion piece (it omits the King's Son title), Nakhtmin is shown with his mother, the Adoratrix of Min, Songstress of Isis, Iuy.[30] This may well be the first wife of Ay who may have borne Nefertiti,[31] remembered in the furnishings of her son's (now lost) tomb-chapel.[32]

As king, Ay took the following titulary (appendix 3):

Horus	*k3-nḫt tḫn-ḫʿw/ḫprw*	Strong bull dazzling of appearances/ manifestations
Nebti	*sḥm-pḥty dr-Stiw*	Great of power, subduer of the Asiatics
Golden Falcon	*ḥq3-m3ʿt sḫpr-t3wy*	Ruler of Maat, who nurtures the Two Lands
Prenomen	*ḫpr-ḫprw-Rʿ iri-M3ʿt*	Manifestation of manifestions of Re, doer of Maat[33]
Nomen	*it-nṯr ʾIy nṯr-ḥq3-W3st*	God's Father Ay, god and ruler of Thebes[34]

Particularly interesting points regarding this list are the mention of Asia/Asiatics in the Nebti-name—perhaps reflecting current troubles in northern Syria—and the fact that two of the epithets ("Doer of Maat" and "God's Father") built into the two cartouche names were ones that had featured in Ay's titulary as a commoner. Both presumably represented policy statements, the latter emphasizing the continuity between the Tutankhamun and Ay regimes.

This also may have lain behind Ay's completion and decoration of the Temple of Nebkheperure in Thebes. The late king is given equal prominence with Ay, who delights in dedicating it to "his son." While this may have reflected simply an affection for Tutankhamun, it was also quite likely a monumental recognition of the absolute dependence of Ay's own status on his being the legal heir of the final blood-scion of the main dynastic line.[35]

The mode of his accession and the events surrounding it would have presented the new king with his first challenge. This was how to deal with the fallout from the Zananzash affair. As we have seen, the Hittite king blamed the Egyptians for his prince's demise, but from a fragmentary draft letter in the Hittite archives[36] it would appear that Ay had attempted to assure Shuppiluliumash of his regime's innocence in the matter. The draft is of a reply to what seems a series of Egyptian letters, and although much is missing, there are enough references to a "son's death," and allegations that the addressee had been responsible for the killing, to link it with the *dénouement* of the affair.

The implication of what can be read is that Ay was trying to assuage the Hittite king's anger and was urging that friendly relations (brotherhood) be maintained; and that Shuppiluliumash rejected his overtures. Rightly or wrongly, Shuppiluliumash continued to blame the Egyptians for Zananzash's death and, presumably after having sent the actual letter to the Egyptian court, "let his anger run away with him and he went to war against Egypt and attacked Egypt"—or rather, Egyptian-controlled territory in northern Syria. There he took Egyptian prisoners who were transported back to Hatti, but they "brought a plague into the land of Hatti. From that day there has been a dying in the midst of the land of Hatti."[37] Among those to die were Shuppiluliumash himself and his successor, Arnuwandash II.

Another matter to be dealt with was that of the dowager queen Ankhesenamun. Any view of what might have been the prevailing situation naturally depends on how far Ay had been aware of, or had acquiesced in, the Hittite candidature. Relations between the young dowager and the aging new king could have ranged from merely uncomfortable to implacably hostile. Unfortunately, only one piece of relevant data exists, a glass finger-ring that bears the prenomen of Ay joined with the cartouche of Ankhesenamun.[38]

This presumably implies a marriage between the two, but Ankhesenamun is never heard of again, and Ay's Great Wife is always the commoner, Tey. However, Ay may have taken an additional wife late in life, perhaps to sire a new heir after Nakhtmin's premature death, as the title God's Father was later added to the title-string of Tutankhamun's old tutor Sennedjem in his tomb, suggesting that he might have come to be father-in-law of the king.[39] Or might Sennedjem actually have been Tey's father? He was another Akhmimi, and his high status could well be explained by such a relationship with Ay. Certainly Sennedjem shared Ay's posthumous opprobrium, as can be seen by the state of his tomb. The main issue would be the relative ages of Sennedjem and Ay, but if Tey were indeed Ay's second wife, she could have been considerably younger than him, making Sennedjem of approximately Ay's generation.

It appears that one of the now-queen's nephews, Ay (B), son of her sister Mutemnub by her husband the judge Nakhtmin (A), was appointed Second Prophet of Amun and First Prophet of Mut, as well as the queen's own steward (fig. 71).[40] However, few other officials can be clearly dated to Ay's reign. Many will doubtless have continued in office from Tutankhamun's regime, and certainly Maya was still treasurer during Horemheb's reign. One would assume that Horemheb remained in a position of power, but no material definitely dating to Ay's reign refers to him: the king depicted in his Saqqara tomb appears throughout to be Tutankhamun. It is possible that the tomb of Ptahemhat-Ty, the high priest of Ptah, might date to Ay's reign rather than Tutankhamun's, and if the unnamed *iry-pʿt imy-r mšʿ* who led Ty's funeral procession were indeed Horemheb (fig. 62),[41] this would be his sole attestation under Ay.

However, given the implications of the *iry-pʿt* title, which during the New Kingdom can imply "crown prince,"[42] it is not

Fig. 71. Block statue of Ay B, Ay's nephew by marriage, Second Prophet of Amun, First Prophet of Mut, and steward of Queen Tey (BMA 67.174.1).

impossible that the figure at the head of the procession was actually Nakhtmin B. As Ay's son, he would indeed have held this position, and was of course also a general, who had actually now advanced to Generalissimo. As such he may well have eclipsed Horemheb in both his civil and military roles following Ay's accession.[43]

Looking at other members of the hierarchy during Ay's reign, apparently a new appointee was Paser, the viceroy of Nubia, who had succeeded his father Huy. The new man is known from a shrine at Gebel el-Shams, near Abu Simbel,[44] and he continued in office under Horemheb.[45] At Thebes, a certain Nay, buried in TT271,[46] held a range of senior titles, including Noble, Count, Chief Physician, God's Father and Beloved of the god, Overseer of Works, Fan Bearer on the Right of the King, and Scribe of the Recruits.[47] All mark him out as a key figure at Ay's court, but his tomb seems to have escaped intentional damage, apart from what seems to have been a half-hearted attack on the king's cartouche.[48]

The Chief Scribe of Amun was one Neferhotep, in whose tomb-chapel (TT49) the king and queen are shown tossing flowers from a balcony.[49] In the north, Ramose, a Royal Scribe and Overseer of the Two Granaries, the royal scribes Meryre and Tjay, together with Re the Chief of the Attendants, are all known from a stela found in the Temple of Isis, Mistress of the Pyramids, at Giza.[50] Two provincial high priests are known: Ibeba at Mendes, from his statue,[51] and Nakhtmin (C) at Akhmim, from his stelae (fig. 72);[52] but nothing is known of the incumbents at the major centers at Thebes and Memphis, unless the

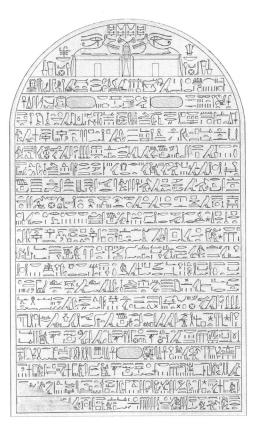

Fig. 72. One of the pair of stelae erected in Ay's fourth regnal year by Nakhtmin C, high priest of Min (Berlin 2074).

aforementioned funeral of the high priest of Ptah, Ptahemhat-Ty, indeed took place under Ay rather than Tutankhamun.[53]

Ay created a rock-cut temple in a spectacular location at el-Salamuni overlooking the city of Akhmim and the surrounding area.[54] His Overseer of Works at Akhmim was a Nakhtmin (Q),[55] who may or may not be identical with the homonymous high priest noted above. Although depicted in the rock temple, he was presumably also responsible for the temple of Min in the city of Akhmim itself. There, an exposure of a gateway of Ramesside date has been accompanied by a number of items of reused sculpture (fig. 73), the remains of at least two colossal kingly statues being datable stylistically to the late Eighteenth Dynasty, though reinscribed for Rameses II. Similarly datable is a colossal standing figure of a queen (fig. 74), in this case reinscribed for Rameses II's daughter Meryetamun E. The face is wholly unlike known images of Ankhesenamun and Mutnodjmet, but can be paralleled by the visages of statues of Mut at Karnak and Luxor that can be dated to Ay's reign (fig. 75).[56] The Akhmim queen is thus almost certainly Tey.[57] Ay's affiliations with Akhmim are also signaled by the mention of "Min of Ipu" in a broken text of an address by nobles to Ay recorded in TT49.[58] This

Fig. 73. The temple gateway area at Akhmim. This revealed late Eighteenth-Dynasty statuary usurped by Rameses II, as well as fragments of relief from the time of Akhenaten.

text also contains a passage that declares to Ay: "How refreshing is [. . .] the hearing of your [. . .]"; interestingly, this is almost exactly the same wording that Ay uses in addressing Akhenaten in his old Amarna tomb.[59] Other provincial building work included a "Temple of Kheperkheperure-irimaat in Abydos" known from the stela of its chief sculptor, Amenemopet,[60] and the final installation of a granite lion begun by Amenhotep III for his Soleb temple, finished by Tutankhamun, but still languishing (presumably in Aswan) at Ay's accession.[61]

In the Memphite area, a stela of Ay was apparently dedicated in the Sekhmet sanctuary in the ancient mortuary temple of Sahure at Abu Sir.[62] Another fragment from a stela of the king turned up in the area of the Palace of Apries at Memphis itself.[63] A Memphite "Estate of Kheperkheperure-irimaat" is known from a stela of its steward Tjutju.[64] At Thebes-East, Ay's principal effort concerned the continuation and completion of the Temple of Nebkheperure in Thebes at Karnak as a joint monument,[65] and produced at least one colossal dyad of Amun and Mut bearing the features of himself and Tey.[66] He continued Tutankhamun's work on the façade of the Great Colonnade at Luxor Temple—but not apparently that of the main walls[67]—and also undertook a restoration in the inner part of the temple,[68] but his names do not survive. On the other hand, at least one of the two dyads of Amun and Mut that now stand in the Colonnade are to be dated to Ay's reign (fig. 75).[69]

At Thebes West, Ay began his memorial temple just north of Medinet Habu, a little to the south of the potential temple sites of his predecessor (figs. 66 and 67). Although equipped with foundation deposits in Ay's name, it was to be usurped and completed by Horemheb, but was later almost completely demolished.[70] Interestingly, Ay's Overseer of Works for the temple was the Akhmimi high priest Nakhtmin C,[71] rather than a more local official.

The other part of Ay's burial installation was his tomb in the West Valley of the Kings, WV23.[72] As noted in Chapter 4, the tomb might have been begun for Tutankhamun, although no definitive evidence— e.g., foundation deposits—has been found. The tomb's plan is clearly attenuated as compared with its original design, which was presumably akin to that of Horemheb's KV57 (fig. 65). Whether this was a result of emergency action on Ay's demise or a planned downsizing is of course a moot point—however, Ay's likely advanced age at accession[73] may have led him to take a conservative approach to providing himself with a royal tomb. Indeed, this may have been the reason for his putative taking over of the tomb from Tutankhamun—to provide himself with a ready-to-use kingly sepulcher.

Only the burial chamber of WV23 was decorated and, like the tomb of Tutankhamun, its decoration was both abbreviated and innovative.[74] Once again the Book of Amduat was cut down to elements of the first hour, with images of the king and gods distributed along one long wall. Alongside some other mythological elements, however, is a double scene of the king spearing a hippopotamus and fowling in a canoe, with Queen Tey looking on (fig. 76). This is unusual in two particular aspects: first, it is the only time that a queen has substantive representation in a king's tomb;[75] second, while the hunting/fowling motif goes back to the Old Kingdom, its use in a burial chamber is not otherwise attested, although it is a standard feature of pre-Amarna Theban private tomb-chapels, and is also known in royal memorial temples.[76] Its frequent modern characterization as a nonroyal feature, perhaps reflecting some ambiguity as to Ay's status, thus misses the point: it is simply in the wrong part of the tomb, paralleling the intrusive mummy-dragging scene in Tutankhamun's burial chamber. As the style of the two tombs' decoration is so similar, a common draftsman is likely[77]—and possibly one who was keen to test the boundaries of what

Fig. 74. Colossal statue at Akhmim, probably made to represent Queen Tey, but later reinscribed for Rameses II's daughter Meryetamun E.

Fig. 75. Dyad of Amun and Mut in the colonnade of Luxor Temple, with the faces of Ay and Tey.

was possible in the post-Amarna climate, which generated many significant changes in mortuary decoration.[78]

The tomb was equipped with a sarcophagus of the same basic design as that of Tutankhamun, with a protective goddess on each corner; a design derived from the royal canopic chests of the middle Eighteenth Dynasty, and the sarcophagus of Akhenaten, which had placed Nefertiti on the corners.[79] As in Tutankhamun's tomb, the head of the sarcophagus was oriented toward the wall that bore the abbreviated Amduat.[80]

The death of Ay occurred at some point after Year 4, IV *ȝḥt*, day 1, which is his latest known date, recorded on the stelae of Nakhtmin C. Its circumstances remain unknown, but in view of the king's age it could well have been from natural causes. However, the key question is what manner of interment was granted to him, given that the figures and names of the king and queen on the walls of WV23 were all mutilated, with some damage also done to the sarcophagus. Its lid was found upside down on the floor, a position not inconsistent with its having been thrown off the coffer by robbers, as is found in other tombs, thus indicating it had actually been used for a burial. On the other hand it has suffered little damage, which might suggest it had never been placed in position but had been propped up against a wall and then tipped over on its back.[81]

Fig. 76. The king and queen hunting and fishing, in the burial chamber of Ay (WV23).

Fig. 77. A knob bearing the name of Ay, found in the tomb of Nefertiry D (QV66: Turin S.5162).

The tomb also contained little in the way of funerary equipment debris, with no trace of shabtis or canopic equipment, fragments of whose fragile alabaster chest survived in most other mid-Eighteenth to mid-Nineteenth Dynasty royal tombs.[82] This might all point to the tomb's not having been used, or to its having been the site of a distinctly perfunctory interment that omitted many items and did not even put the sarcophagus lid in place. On the other hand, that a burial was made is suggested by the presence of a gilt copper rosette (probably the adornment of a funerary pall) and various wooden fragments from funerary statuettes, together with some Eighteenth Dynasty pottery.[83]

One might thus suggest that to ensure the legality of his accession, Ay's successor carried out the burial of the old king, but with the minimum expense of effort and resources, and perhaps then diverting much of Ay's equipment for rework, in much the same way as Neferneferuaten's had been a decade before. However, as we shall see,[84] Ay's monuments soon afterward began to be mutilated, and probably at the same time his tomb was entered and desecrated.[85] Some of the debris was perhaps pilfered by persons charged with its destruction, as items (including embossed gold foil from pieces of furniture, and perhaps even a chariot) bearing Ay's name ended up in a pit tomb (KV58) in the main Valley of the Kings.[86] Whether the mummy was destroyed or quietly re-buried in obscurity will probably never be known.[87]

Ay, together with the other kings who had reigned since the end of Amenhotep III's reign, was written out of history: the monumental chronological offering lists of Sethy I and Rameses II at Abydos[88] and Tjenry at Saqqara[89] all jump straight from Amenhotep to Horemheb. By the reign of Rameses II, the years of all their reigns had been formally reallocated to Horemheb.[90] All the more strange, then, that in the tomb of Rameses II's Great Wife Nefertiry D was found a faience knob bearing Ay's cartouche (fig. 77).[91] This could of course be a stray, or part of an old piece of furniture on which the name had been overlooked; however its presence might suggest some familial link between the disgraced king and the queen.[92] Beyond this little can be said.

7 THE HAWK IN FESTIVAL

W hile the career of his erstwhile colleague Ay can be traced back to the early years of Akhenaten, Horemheb first appears unequivocally on the scene during the reign of Tutankhamun. Some have wondered whether he might previously have served Akhenaten under another name, although Horus was never unacceptable at Amarna. Nevertheless, General Paatenemheb, who began tomb TA24 there,[1] has sometimes been proposed to be Horemheb in an earlier guise. That there may have been some stages of promotion is suggested by the clear series of four constructional phases seen in Horemheb's Saqqara tomb (fig. 80), which ultimately doubled the size of the tomb; but these cannot be tied down to the evolution of his titulary.[2]

Fig. 78. The restoration text of Horemheb in the upper colonnade of the temple of Hatshepsut at Deir el-Bahari.

In practice, the origins of the man who became Tutankhamun's regent, and would ultimately become king himself, are obscure. In his restoration inscription in the Upper Colonnade of the temple of Hatshepsut at Deir el-Bahari (fig. 78),[3] Horemheb calls Thutmose III "father of his fathers," but whether this might indicate a remote claim to royal blood, or just a view of the inherent unity of the monarchical succession, is uncertain. Otherwise, our principal source of evidence is Horemheb's long Coronation Inscription. The most complete version is on the rear of a Turin statue (fig. 79),[4] with fragmentary

Fig. 79. The Coronation
Statue of Horemheb
(Turin C.1379).

examples on a Memphis stela[5] and on a Karnak doorway of Amenhotep III.[6] The text opens with Horemheb's royal titles, in which he is described as "beloved of Horus of Hutnesu" (modern Kom el-Ahmar Sawaris in northern Middle Egypt),[7] presumably his home town. It then goes on to describe Horemheb as born with divine protection, recognized as special since childhood, and destined for kingship. The key actor is "Horus," who foresees the time when he will hand over the kingship to Horemheb, and therefore:

> distinguished his son (Horemheb) in the sight of the entire people, for he wished to widen his stride until the day should come of his receiving his office . . . and the king was content with his dealings, and rejoicing at the choosing of him. He set him up as to be chief spokesman of the land in order to make firm the laws of both banks as Noble (iry-pʿt) of this entire land. He was unique, without an equal . . . . When he was summoned before the sovereign, the palace having fallen into rage, he opened his mouth and answered the king and made him happy with the speech of his mouth . . . . Now he governed the Two Lands for many years . . . . The great ones of the Nine Bows appealed to him, south as well as north, their arms outstretched at his approach and they paid honour to his face as (to) a god . . . . Prosperity and health were prayed for on his behalf: Assuredly he is the father of both banks, with the excellent wisdom by the gift of god to make fast [the laws of the land?].
>
> Many [days] passed over these things, the eldest son of Horus being chief spokesman and prince of this whole land; then this noble god, Horus of Hutnesu, his heart desired to establish his son upon his throne of eternity . . . . Then Horus proceeded rejoicing to Thebes, the city of the lord of eternity, his son in his embrace, to Karnak, in order to lead him into the presence of Amun to assign to him his office of king and make his period (of office) . . . .

The idea of a predestined ruler looked after by his god since childhood is a longstanding one and appears in the myth and political propaganda of numerous cultures. An issue in assessing the whole text is the way one should interpret the various references to "Horus," as it appears that more than one individual may be involved. "Horus of Hutnesu" is named twice, while "Horus son of Isis" also appears in the introductory section—but a simple

"Horus" appears frequently elsewhere in the text: is he either of these, one of the other Horuses, or the reigning king, who can of course also be Horus?

Given Horemheb's subsequent treatment of his predecessors, one wonders if the text is being intentionally ambiguous. The text quoted above certainly describes Horemheb's status under Tutankhamun, but is it stating that power was bestowed on him by the king himself (i.e., Horus) or via a theological justification for a *coup d'état*, either against Neferneferuaten or directly after her death?[8] Or do we have here some constructive ambiguity? The "palace rage" passage is also intriguing—is this a reference to a particular incident (under which king?), or is it a rhetorical flourish implying that if things were going badly, only Horemheb could soothe the king's mood? On a slightly different tack, could the section regarding the Nine Bows be linked to the representations of captive foreigners in Horemheb's Saqqara tomb (fig. 44)?

It is the final part of this section, describing the way in which Horemheb actually came to the throne, where the potential constructive ambiguity becomes most frustrating. Horemheb is described as $s\!\!^3\ sms(w)\ n\ \d{H}r$, "eldest son of Horus," which is clearly intended to parallel the title $s\!\!^3\text{-}nsw\ smsw$, "Eldest King's Son" that had designated the heir to the throne since the beginning of the Eighteenth Dynasty.[9] But is this "Horus" a god or a king—and if so, which king?

Fundamentally, this boils down to whether Horemheb had been nominated by Ay as his heir (presumably following the premature death of Nakhtmin)[10] or once again is claiming divine sanction for a seizure of power. The immediately following reference to "Horus of Hutnesu" as initiating his elevation to the throne might favor the latter interpretation, but the next sentence goes back to a noncommittal "Horus," who takes him to Karnak during the Opet festival "to assign to him his office of king." Is this the king using the occasion of the Opet to appoint Horemheb as his coregent, or is Horemheb using the Opet festival as a suitable backdrop for consolidating his seizure of power? The purposely ruined state of Nakhtmin's statue (fig. 70) indicates hostility between Horemheb and Nakhtmin, but was that on the basis of a power struggle at Ay's death, or simply part of the retrospective posthumous persecution of Ay and his associates? We will return to this below when considering the origins of Horemheb's queen.

The Coronation Inscription goes on to describe, in a very flowery manner, the Coronation of Horemheb during the Opet festival at Thebes— the annual celebration that is the subject of the reliefs inscribed on the walls of the Great Colonnade at Luxor.[11] The ceremonies included the announcement of his titulary (appendix 3):

Horus	*k3-nḥt spd-sḥrw*	Strong bull penetrating of plans
Nebti	*wr-bi3wt m 'Ipt-swt*	Great of marvels in Karnak
Golden Falcon	*ḥrw-ḥr-m3ᶜt shpr-t3wy*	Contented with Maat, who nurtures the Two Lands
Prenomen	*ḏsr-ḫprw-Rᶜ stp-n-Rᶜ*	Divine of manifestations of Re, chosen of Re
Nomen	*ḥr-m-ḥb mr-n-'Imn*	Horemheb, beloved of Amun

The formulation of the Golden Falcon name closely recalls that of Ay, with only the first word changed, suggesting a common policy statement underlying both names. However, the other names are new, although Horemheb follows Ay in building permanent epithets into both cartouche names, something that would become a particular feature of royal titularies during Ramesside and Third Intermediate Period times.

The inscription then continues:

> When the festival of the Southern Opet was over . . . his person sailed downstream with the statue of (Re-)Horakhty and set this land in order, organizing it as had been in the time of Re. He renewed the temples of the gods from the marshes of the Delta to Aswan and fashioned all their images, distinguished from what had been before and surpassing in beauty through what he had done to them, so that Re rejoiced when he saw them (since) he found them ruined from a former time. He (re)erected their temples and created their statues, each in their exact shape, out of every costly stone. He sought out the precincts of the gods that were in ruins in this land and refounded them as they had been since the First Time and instituted for them regular offerings every day. Every vessel of their temples was made in gold and silver and he equipped them with *waab*-priests and lector-priests from the pick of the army, assigning to them fields and herds, equipped on all sides . . . .

This coda echoes in many ways the Restoration Stela of Tutankhamun, and represents a clear statement of a continuity in the policy of restoring temples

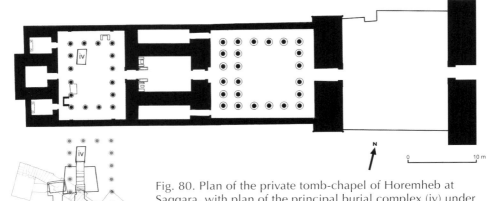

Fig. 80. Plan of the private tomb-chapel of Horemheb at Saqqara, with plan of the principal burial complex (iv) under the inner courtyard. The tomb first comprised just this inner courtyard, its chapels, and a forecourt; the latter was later converted into a corridor flanked by statue chambers, with a new forecourt added. Pillars were subsequently added to this, together with a pylon gateway. A further pylon was ultimately added even farther east.

that had fallen on hard times during Akhenaten's reign—not surprisingly, given Horemheb's senior role under Tutankhamun. Restoration inscriptions in Horemheb's name are thus present in various locations around Thebes, including some where restorations of Tutankhamun are either usurped or even re-restored.[12]

On his Turin statue, Horemheb is accompanied by his queen, Mutnodjmet. Her origins have been much debated, in particular whether she might be identical with the sister of Nefertiti.[13] If Horemheb were indeed Nefertiti's brother-in-law it would certainly explain his position in the post-Akhenaten hierarchy, even more so if the speculation making Ay the father of the sisters is correct. As Ay's son-in-law, Horemheb would also be his obvious heir following any premature death of Nakhtmin. On the other hand, Horemheb would also be very well placed to embark on a palace intrigue to supplant his putative brother-in-law in the succession. Unfortunately, insufficient data exist to go much further, although it must be said that the identity between Nefertiti's sister and Horemheb's wife is probably the most attractive solution. Against Ay's parentage one could cite Mutnodjmet's lack of the title of King's Daughter, but given the treatment meted out to Ay, this may well have been a connection Horemheb would not have wished to publicize!

As to when Horemheb might have married Mutnodjmet, no data is available.[14] That he might have had an earlier wife, Amenia, has been suggested on the basis of a mention of a Chantress of Amun of that name on a pillar in Horemheb's private tomb at Saqqara.[15] However, her link to Horemheb is unclear (was she mother, sister, or other relation?) and the general assumption that she preceded Mutnodjmet as his spouse is without real basis.[16] Likewise the view that burial chamber iv/F in the tomb (fig. 80) belonged to this putative "first, or nonroyal, wife of Horemheb"[17] is also pure assumption. Thus, it is quite possible that Mutnodjmet had married Horemheb early in his career[18] and is the wife shown with Horemheb on the various statues from his private tomb (e.g., fig. 81).[19]

Fig. 81. Dyad of Horemheb and an unnamed wife, from his Saqqara tomb (Luxor Museum).

Nevertheless, it seems clear that a lady[20] close to Horemheb was buried in or near chamber iv/F of the tomb during the reign of Ay: a number of votive plaques bearing that king's name were found in shaft iv,[21] while seals used to close the access corridor to iv/F might preserve a version of Ay's prenomen.[22] Wine jars marked with "Year 1" found in the shaft[23] could belong to Ay—or potentially Tutankhaten.[24]

As queen, Mutnodjmet is known from a number of monuments.[25] In three dimensions, apart from the aforementioned Turin dyad, there are: the base of a standing dyad found at Karnak;[26] a fragmentary single statue from her husband's private tomb;[27] a fragmentary standing colossus from Dendara (figs. 82 and 83);[28] and (probably) a head from Horemheb's memorial temple.[29] Mutnodjmet's figure also appeared alongside Horemheb's leg on the pair of colossi that flank the gate of Pylon X at Karnak (fig. 84).[30] Her name also replaced that of Ankhesenamun in the label-text to the Queen's Barge in the Opet reliefs on the east wall of the Great Colonnade at Luxor,[31] but curiously not on Tutankhamun's Restoration Stela, where Ankhesenamun's image was instead erased. Mutnodjmet also once appeared with her husband making offerings in the tomb of the royal scribe Roy (TT255).[32]

Fig. 82. Remains of a colossal statue of Mutnodjmet at Dendara.

The Dendara colossus gives Mutnodjmet the title of *ḥmt-nṯr*, God's Wife, making her one of the relatively few queens of the second part of the New Kingdom to bear this title.[33] A further intimation as to her apparent inheritance of the kind of enhanced queenly status seen in the case of Tiye and Nefertiti is made apparent by the motif on her side of the throne of the Turin dyad, where she appears as a winged sphinx of unique style (fig. 85). Such representations of a royal lady were not common, and mark a continuation of a series of "powerful" representations of queens[34] that begins with Tiye A who is shown in sphinx form at Sedeinga,[35] where she combines with Tefnut "great of fearsomeness," incarnate in the sphinx.[36] Along similar lines, Nefertiti appears in the pose of smiting a cowering enemy well before her elevation to the kingship as Neferneferuaten (fig. 30).

It has been proposed[37] that Mutnodjmet was buried in Horemheb's original burial complex at Saqqara.[38] This is based on the discovery, on the rim of the shaft leading into the burial chamber, of the remains of the skeleton of a middle-aged woman, mingled with those of a foetus or newborn, the implication being that the woman had died in childbirth.[39] The woman had previously gone through a number of difficult deliveries, possibly with high resultant blood loss and anemia; she had also suffered from severe dental disease and was almost toothless at death. In favor of this identification—including her usage of the main burial chamber (iv/P) of the tomb—is the presence of fragments of a canopic(?) jar of Mutnodjmet in the *other* burial chamber (iv/F) in the complex,[40] and of the aforementioned statue of the queen in the tomb's superstructure. This putative interment of Mutnodjmet has been placed in Year 13 of Horemheb on the basis of two so-dated wine jar fragments found nearby,[41] although others dating to Year 1 (of Tutankhaten—or conceivably Ay) were also found in the shaft complex.[42] A canopic jar generally regarded as belonging to Horemheb's Mutnodjmet was purchased by the British Museum in 1870 (fig. 86);[43] its provenance is unknown, although a label affixed at some point to the jar reads, intriguingly, "Memphis."[44]

The true condition of the country at Horemheb's succession is an interesting question. A text (the Edict of Horemheb), preserved on a stela fragment from Abydos[45] and a broken stela standing against the north face of the west tower of the Pylon X at Karnak (fig. 87),[46] paints a fairly lurid picture of governmental corruption. It speaks of property being summarily expropriated, slaves taken away to work for tax collectors, soldiers embezzling cattle hides, the seizing of foodstuffs ostensibly in the king's name, and various other corrupt acts by state officials. The text presents Horemheb's disgust at the situation as being such that he wrote out the resulting edict with his own hand. It provides for exemplary punishments to be imposed on guilty parties, such as cutting off the nose and subsequent exile to the northeastern frontier zone of Tjaru,[47] inflicting a hundred blows and five open wounds, and even the death penalty. The text ends with the king appointing officials to supervise

Fig. 83. Text on the back pillar of the Dendara colossus. Mutnodjmet's ownership can be determined by a combination of the remains of the Mut-sign at the top of the cartouches, and the overall style of the figure, which is typical of the late Eighteenth Dynasty.

Fig. 84. The north face of Pylon X at Karnak, erected by Horemheb; the colossi have figures of Mutnodjmet against their legs. The statues were later usurped by Rameses II and Nefertiry D.

Fig. 85. Mutnodjmet as a sphinx, on the side of her throne on the Coronation Statue (fig. 79).

the implementation of the decree, marking its issue by a public appearance that features the distribution of food to the assembled multitudes, and allegedly calling each person forward by name to receive their share. It ends with the exhortation: "Listen to these commands which my person has made for the first time governing the whole land, when my person remembered these cases of oppression that occurred before this land."

As always with such texts, it is difficult to decide how true a picture is painted. The motif of a king coming to the throne at a dark time and resolving the situation by his action and wisdom is a common one in royal texts, and is also seen in Tutankhamun's Restoration Stela. The question is how truly dark was that time, and how far it was artificially darkened for political effect, as background for what might have been a simple evolutionary set of reforms?[48]

The development of Horemheb's attitude to his predecessors is seen most instructively at Karnak, where Ay's names were first carefully erased from the Temple of Nebkheperure in Thebes, presumably with the intention of replacing them with those of Horemheb, while those of Tutankhamun himself were left intact (fig. 52). Plans were then changed and the dismantling of the building was begun. Some of the architraves had apparently already disappeared into the core of Horemheb's Pylon II when all the images and names of both Ay and Tutankhamun remaining on those of parts of the building still accessible were mutilated.[49] This seems to have coincided with the demolition of the inner parts of the temple, with the images of Tutankhamun and Ay both being attacked before being consigned to the construction of Pylons IX and X and adjacent walls.[50] This would suggest that while hostility toward Ay was manifest from fairly early on in Horemheb's reign, the decision to place Tutankhamun among the damned seems to have been taken rather later.

Fig. 86. A canopic jar of Mutnodjmet (BM EA36635).

The situation described in the Edict of Horemheb would thus seem to be a statement of the official view of the reign of Ay. Whether it was as corrupt a period as described is of course a moot point, but evidence suggesting that Tutankhamun's tomb was robbed within a very short time—if not days—of the funeral[51] would certainly suggest that things were not all well during the first part of Ay's regime in the necropolis administration at Thebes. Of course, administrative dislocation would have been an inevitable concomitant of the political uncertainties surrounding the "Zananzash Affair."[52] In any case its description in these terms is perhaps an argument in favor of the view that Ay's reign saw Horemheb's political eclipse. If Horemheb had remained in the center of affairs under Ay, it seems unlikely that he would have painted the situation in a way that would have reflected on him by association as one of the body of Ay's officials. Thus we could see the reign of Ay as Horemheb's wilderness years, which allowed him, nevertheless, to present himself as one who could make a clean start after the alleged rampant corruption of Ay's regime.

There may, however, have been issues with the reliability of necropolis officials some years into Horemheb's reign. In Year 8, it was necessary for the treasurer Maya and the steward of Thebes Thutmose to restore the robbed burial of Thutmose IV:[53] robbery in the Valley of the Kings would have been difficult without some kind of inside help.

One wonders whether these robberies in the Valley of the Kings were linked in any way with the presence there of workmen engaged on the construction of Horemheb's own tomb (KV57: fig. 65).[54] In any case, the Valley of the Kings workmen's community at Deir el-Medina seems to have been subject to some kind of restructuring in Year 7, as in that year an allocation of tomb space in the village necropolis had taken place,[55] implying new arrivals. This may have been a result of a need for a new mix of skills in the community, as Horemheb's tomb differs fundamentally from all earlier Valley of the Kings sepulchers in being decorated in relief rather than flat paint. Not only would this require sculptors (who were not needed in the earlier tombs),[56] but also it was a far more laborious technique that entirely changed the scheduling of tomb construction. Rather than the decoration being capable of at least partial execution after the placement of the mummy in the tomb,[57] it should be fully complete by the king's demise. That the new approach was not fully bedded in is probably indicated by the fact that the decoration of Horemheb's tomb was never completed, in spite of only the principal rooms being earmarked for adornment.[58] On the other hand, that lessons were swiftly learned is indicated by the fact that, soon after Horemheb's death, the tomb of Sethy I could be carved and painted throughout almost its entire length[59] within his eleven-year[60] reign.

To complement his Valley of the Kings tomb, Horemheb took over the doubtless unfinished memorial temple of Ay, enlarging it through the addition of a peristyle court and an extra (third) pylon (fig. 66).[61] Ay's statues

Fig. 87. Stela behind Pylon X at Karnak bearing the Edict of Horemheb.

Fig. 88. View of the ruins of the mortuary temple of Horemheb; in the background is the outer enclosure wall of Medinet Habu.

were all usurped, including a pair of quartzite pieces that have often been identified as being originally made for Tutankhamun,[62] and new ones were manufactured; only a few fragments of the wall reliefs have survived from the devastated site (figs. 66 and 88).

Back at his old tomb at Saqqara, little was done to mark Horemheb's elevation to the purple except for the addition of a uraeus to the brow of most of his figures in the tomb (fig. 89).[63] In this approach he was followed by subsequent individuals in the same kind of situation, e.g., Merenptah[64] and Messuy/Amenmeses.[65] The only apparent addition of Horemheb's kingly cartouches in the tomb was to former images of Tutankhamun,[66] with the result that Horemheb is effectively twice shown rewarding himself!

Also at Saqqara, Horemheb constructed a tomb (D/E) that was ultimately used for the interment of the two sacred Apis bulls that died during his reign.[67] They were the successors of the bull that had died under Tutankhamun,[68] but the dates of their deaths are unknown. The above-ground chapel preserved a block in the king's name, below which lay two chambers. Apis IV was placed in the decorated chamber D, the first such room known in an Apis tomb, painted in a style that closely recalls the tombs of Tutankhamun and Ay, suggesting that the same artists may have been employed. The room had been entirely cleared out by robbers, with the exception of a canopic jar lid. However, the roughly cut adjoining chamber E of Apis V was intact.

Year 13 dates on amphorae found both here and in the Saqqara tomb.[115] However, a case for a substantially higher figure can be made on the basis of the text of Mose, the Scribe of the Treasury of Ptah, dating to the reign of Rameses II, in which he recounts a long legal battle that stretched back into the last decades of the Eighteenth Dynasty.[116] One of the key points in the narrative inscribed in Mose's tomb at Saqqara is dated to "this day, Year 59 under the person of the Dual King Djeser-kheperure . . . ."[117] The date is clearly written, without any scope for confusion, but there can be no chance that Horemheb really ruled that long.

The only explanation for such a high number would be that the Ramesside scribe, wishing to avoid any need to refer to the reigns of now non-persons Akhenaten, Tutankhamun, and Ay, retrospectively allocated their aggregate years to Horemheb.[118]

Fig. 94. Statue of the vizier Paramessu. From Karnak (Cairo JE44861).

Adding together their known years (seventeen, nine, and four) we arrive at around thirty to thirty-one[119] years, which when subtracted from the fifty-nine would place Mose's legal event in Horemheb's Year 28/29.[120] On the other hand, such an interpretation has been challenged on the basis that other texts of the same period do not seem squeamish about giving dates within the reign of Akhenaten, who is referred to therein as "the rebel,"[121] and that real years of Horemheb were certainly quoted in Ramesside documents.[122] However, it seems hardly likely that a scribe would erroneously have written such a high number in place of the correct "*19" or suchlike, especially in a text whose internal chronology was an important factor. It is also possible that the approach taken to dating varied according to context; the Mose inscription thus remains *prima facie* evidence for a minimum reign for Horemheb of not far off thirty years.

Fig. 95. Upper part of the Year 400 Stela carved during the reign of Rameses II, which apparently refers back to a celebration of an anniversary of the god Seth under Horemheb. The protagonist is a vizier Sethy, presumably the son of Paramessu and later king as Sethy I. From San el-Hagar (Tanis: Cairo JE60539).

Such a figure is not inconsistent with some interpretations of a rather cryptic graffito from the memorial temple of Horemheb, which reads: "Year 27, I *šmw*, day 9, the day on which entered Horemheb, LPH, beloved of Amun, who hates his enemies and loves [. . .]."[123] This has been taken variously as recording the arrival of Horemheb's mummy for its funeral,[124] a visit by the living king, or the movement of a cult image of the dead king during the reign of Rameses II.[125] The way in which the text refers to Horemheb is certainly supportive of the last option,[126] as a living king would generally be simply "his person," while the prenomen would otherwise be expected. In any case, the graffito cannot safely be used to bolster a three-decade reign for Horemheb.

This leaves the 28/29 year minimum calculated from the text of Mose against the highest recorded figure of Year 14. The figures in the extant copies of the early Ptolemaic chronicle of Manetho are of little help: the text relating to the Eighteenth/Nineteenth Dynasty transition is horribly corrupt in all surviving editions, giving two kings who might be Horemheb, with widely varying lengths of reign.[127]

The Year 14 has been argued to be Horemheb's last on the basis of its occurrence on amphorae that formed part of his funerary equipment.[128]

However, it seems suspicious that the date occurs in a single group with amphora fragments from Year 13, a vintage that occurs in *both* tombs built by Horemheb: did the king and queen die within a short time of each other?[129] On the other hand, wine placed in a tomb could actually be from a vintage considerably earlier than that of the year of the interment: for example, Tutankhamun's tomb had wine dating from as far back as Year 31 of Amenhotep III.[130] On this basis, it might rather be suggested that in Years 13/14 a large batch of those years' vintages was laid aside for use in royal interments, and perhaps even pre-positioned in storerooms within the tombs.[131] Indeed, the fact that the Year 14 wine was of "good" quality and the Year 13 of "ordinary" quality may favor the bulk purchase solution. Thus, the amphorae's Year 14 should probably not be regarded as having any direct implications as to the dates of either the Saqqara or the Theban interments, apart from showing that they can only have happened *after* Years 13/14.

A potential item of evidence in support of a three-decade reign for Horemheb is an ostracon from Deir el-Medina that indicates a year-change

Fig. 96. Horemheb's Overseer of the Granaries, Amenemopet, as depicted in the tomb of Roy (TT255).

in an unknown reign (from Year 26 to 27) between IV *prt* 28 and I *šmw* 13.[132] This does not correspond to the known accession date of any known king with a reign of a quarter century or more.[133]

On the other hand, a letter written by Mininiwy, Chief of Medjay, probably during the second decade of the reign of Rameses II,[134] states that Mininiwy had been in the service of the vizier Khay since Year 7 of Horemheb.[135] If Horemheb did indeed reign for ~30 years, this would give Mininiwy an active career that would extend over 23+1+11+15+x years—probably something in excess of five decades. This is indeed a long career, and might be used to bolster arguments for a short reign for Horemheb.[136] However, it is a single documented occurrence in a culture where jobs could indeed be held for life, and should not be granted excessive weight in the argument.[137]

The unfinished state of Horemheb's Theban tomb has also been cited in favor of a short reign.[138] However, as we have seen above, this can be accounted for by the major change in decorative technique seen in that tomb and the reorganization of the Deir el-Medina workmen's community, both of which could have badly interfered with work. There are also few private tombs at Thebes datable with certainty to his reign[139]—but relatively few tombs anywhere in the necropolis are datable on other than subjective stylistic grounds, and there is a range of presumed late Eighteenth/early Nineteenth Dynasty sepulchers that could quite easily fall within his reign.

One could also cite the considerable building achievements of Horemheb in favor of a long reign, along with the fact that two Apis bulls were buried during his tenure of the throne. However, Sethy I, during his bare decade on the throne, seems to have achieved at least as much as, if not more than Horemheb, while the vagaries of bovine mortality make the second metric difficult to validate.[140]

The question of Horemheb's reign length thus remains not susceptible to a definitive conclusion. However, the evidence of the inscription of Mose would suggest that around three decades is more likely than the lower figure of about half this, proposed on the basis of the amphorae fragments from his tomb. Either way, his reign was regarded as significant by posterity through his being acknowledged as the first legitimate ruler since the days of Amenhotep III.

As such, Horemheb appears among revered former kings in a number of tomb-chapels at Deir el-Medina. In Ramose i's TT7 he is seen in the distinguished company of Amenhotep I, Ahmes-Nefertiry and—less often—Thutmose IV,[141] and he appears in Penbuy and Kasa's TT10 with the first two named and his own successor, Rameses I (fig. 97).[142] Indeed, Horemheb

Fig. 97. Scenes from the shrine of the tomb-chapel of Penbuy and Kasa (TT10). The right wall (top) shows the dead and deified Sethy I, Rameses I, and Horemheb adored by Kasa and his son; on the left wall these kings are joined by Amenhotep I and Ahmes-Nefertiry in receiving the offerings of Penbuy and his brother.

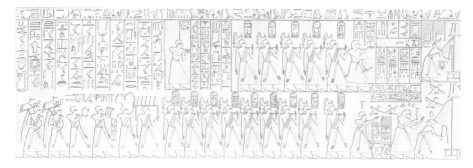

Fig. 98. At the Ramesseum, Horemheb is one of the series of deified kings whose images are carried in procession during the Festival of Min. From the right of the top register they are Thutmose I, Amenhotep I, Ahmose I, Montjuhotep II, Menes, Rameses II, Sethy I, Rameses I, Horemheb, Amenhotep III, Thutmose IV, Amenhotep II, Thutmose III, and Thutmose II, reflecting the new canon of kings that excluded Akhenaten and his immediate successors.

may even be named in the Saite Period tomb of Pedamenopet (TT33), although the orthography of the cartouche is very strange.[143] On royal monuments, Horemheb's statue is carried in procession alongside those of a range of Eighteenth and Nineteenth Dynasty kings, plus First Dynasty founder Menes and Eleventh Dynasty reunifier Montjuhotep II, in the festival of Min as depicted in Rameses II's memorial temple (fig. 98),[144] and that of Rameses III at Medinet Habu.[145] Horemheb is also paired with Montjuhotep on an ostracon, thus indicating that his reign was regarded as a significant era in the broader sweep of Egyptian history.[146]

A posthumous cult of Horemheb was carried on in his memorial temple at Thebes, although for how long is unclear. The previously discussed "Year 27" graffito most probably belongs to Rameses II's reign and relates to Horemheb's cult during that reign, while the continued functioning of the temple as an economic entity is attested in Year 27 of Rameses III.[147] However, the temple was subsequently demolished, a number of its blocks (together with those from other West Theban sanctuaries) being shipped across the river as raw material for the construction of the temple of Khonsu at Karnak.[148] This may have begun toward the end of Rameses III's reign and continued into the early Twenty-first Dynasty.[149]

A cult of Horemheb was also maintained at the Saqqara tomb, where a pair of statues of the canine Anubis was added to the Statue Room, with plinths that depicted Pehefnefer, the Lector Priest of Horemheb, and his family.[150] These seem to date to the reign of Rameses II, and may be linked to the foundation of the tomb of that king's sister Tia on a directly adjoining site.[151] There is also in Late Period a god named Horemheb, the personal name also being popular in Ptolemaic times.[152] Whether this deity is the king, some deified hero, or simply a form of the god Horus is unfortunately unclear, although the gap between the last attestation of the king's cult and the appearance of the god makes the king the least likely candidate.[153]

8 SUNSET

Whether the vizier Paramessu took royal titles only on the death of Horemheb or in advance of this is not wholly clear. The remains of a miniature obelisk bear names of both Horemheb and Rameses I,[1] but whether this marks a coregency, a memorializing by Rameses I of his predecessor, or a monument whose manufacture spanned the change of reign, is unclear.

Either way, the short reign of Rameses I and the accession of his son Sethy I marked the beginning of a new era, with a royal family not apparently linked to the now discredited Eighteenth Dynasty line. Lavish provision for Amun-Re and the traditional gods was now fully reinstitutionalized; Akhenaten and his immediate successors were eliminated from the king-lists and the heretic's temples relegated to mere filling material for use in new structures to the glory of the old gods. Yet things were not the same as they had been prior to the institution of the "solar experiment," back in the days of Amenhotep III.

The increased visibility of the royal family so energetically promoted under Akhenaten continued, and was even expanded under the new dynasty. For the first time ever, royal princes started to be represented in temples by virtue of their status as the king's offspring alone. This contrasts with the Eighteenth Dynasty situation where, for example, crown prince Thutmose appeared with Amenhotep III in an Apis chapel through being high priest of Ptah, not as heir to the throne. In contrast, in Sethy I's Abydos temple, we find crown prince Rameses alongside his father twice in the Corridor of Kings by virtue of that status alone (fig. 99).

135

Fig. 99. Sethy I and crown prince Rameses in the Corridor of Kings at Abydos.

This is taken a step further by Rameses II himself, who was not only shown at Abydos alongside his eldest son Amenhirkopshef A, but adorned many of his building projects with great processions of his sons and daughters, a motif never previously seen (fig. 100);[2] and also constructed a catacomb tomb for some of his sons.[3] In addition, images of sons and daughters of the king become a standard feature of the sides of the back pillars of royal statues. This presentation continues through the Ramesside Period, with the motif of processions of princes and princesses picked up by Hrihor in the Khonsu temple at Karnak to demonstrate his self-proclaimed royalty.[4] The underlying change in the conception of individual members of the royal family may well have led toward the upheavals within the royal family after Merenptah's death and during the last years of Rameses III.[5]

The broader decoration of temples is also changed by the Amarna experience. The kind of whole-wall tableaux seen in Rameses II's Qadesh reliefs are not something generally seen in the pre-Amarna era, and can be traced back directly to the battle reliefs of Tutankhamun and Horemheb, created by artists trained during the Amarna era.[6] The kind of animation seen in these battle reliefs, and later those of Rameses III at Medinet Habu, is also something that can clearly be traced back to Amarna. More subtly, the language of the public inscriptions of Akhenaten slips from Middle Egyptian toward Late Egyptian, an approach which is continued by the Ramesside pharaohs.

Given that the post-Amarna period is notionally one of a return to religious orthodoxy, it is instructive to observe what happens in the most personal of religious spheres, that of the tomb. We have already noted that

Fig. 100. Part of the procession of sons of Rameses II in the forecourt of Luxor Temple.

royal burial chambers undergo a fundamental change in both the technique and content of their decorations under Akhenaten's immediate successors,[7] but a shift of possibly greater import is seen in private tomb-chapels of the post-Amarna era. Instead of their decorative schemes being dominated by the so-called daily life repertoire so typical of the earlier Eighteenth Dynasty and earlier, Ramesside chapels shift the emphasis from the (nominally at least) earthly realm to that of the gods. Scenes relating to the individual's career become relatively rare, while agricultural scenes decrease dramatically in number. Instead, scenes of funerary ritual abound, with depictions of the adoration of deities by the deceased, and extracts from the funerary books that were previously appropriate only to burial chambers.[8]

Thus, the "counter-reformation" that followed the death of Akhenaten, while terminating the monotheistic Atenist experiment, in no way returned Egypt to the *status quo ante*. There had been an underlying change, which the demolition of the monuments of Akhenaten and the erasure of the Amarna kings from the record could not undo. Indeed, it is not clear how far the persecution of the memory of Amarna kings was simply a result of Akhenaten's persecution of Amun, and how far it was inflamed by the new dynasty's desire to emphasize its legitimacy—something that may have lain behind its promotion of the wider royal family.

However, the latter aspect can be overemphasized. There have been attempts to explain the attacks on the memory of Akhenaten in terms of illegitimacy rather than heresy, but these arguments, often on the basis of the nonroyal birth of Queen Tiye, are based on an obsolete understanding of the royal succession and as such have doubtful validity. Ultimately, political imperatives will have trumped any philosophical issues: the rewriting of history at the end of a time of troubles is rarely "fair." Generally, an attempt is made to draw a line under the problematic period with most protagonists expunged from the record. Ultimate devotion to Amun was clearly no barrier to the wholesale usurpation of Tutankhamun's monuments; similarly, Nefertiti's later role as an Amun-tolerating (if not Amun-devoted!) King Neferneferuaten was no barrier to her names and figures sharing her late husband's fate. Smenkhkare fell into very much the same category as Tutankhamun, with his unnaming in KV55 perhaps to be seen as part of a nuanced *damnatio* that left his body intact at a time when Akhenaten's may well have been destroyed. This kind of thinking probably lay behind a number of cases where restorations of figures of Amun and other anthropomorphic deities carried out under Tutankhamun were re-restored by Sethy I, apparently in order to rid the figures of their distinctive Tutankhamunesque features.[9]

It is of course the height of irony that, after this intensive campaign to expunge them from the annals of Egypt, the Amarna pharaohs are today probably the most recognized of all the country's ancient rulers. Indeed, the mask of Tutankhamun and the Berlin bust of Nefertiti are among the most iconic images in the world, while discussion of Akhenaten, his beliefs and activities, can provoke a level of passion that is unusual regarding a man dead for over three millennia.[10] Although the sun set on Akhenaten's vision at the end of the fourteenth century BC, in the twenty-first century AD the names of the heretic and his family are household words in countries unheard of while they themselves trod the Earth.

NOTES

Introduction: Sunrise

1 Cf. Pamminger 1993; Bickel 2002.
2 Dodson 2002b: 58–61.
3 Cf. Johnson 1998: 80–94 ("fourth style").
4 Dodson 1990; 1991; Maystre 1992: 270–72[62–66]; Wildung 1998.
5 Cf. Robins 1987.
6 Cf. Strudwick 1985.
7 Only two royal sons are known during the Twelfth Dynasty (cf. Dodson and Hilton 2004: 93–94, 96).
8 Louvre minature shrine E8074 (Porter and Moss 1974–81: 46; Zivie 1976: 52–55; Dodson 1990: 92[5].
9 Using the designation of homonyms published in Dodson and Hilton 2004.
10 Gardiner 1952: 15, pl. ii[57]; Dodson 1990: 92[7].
11 pBM EA10056 (Pasquali 2007).
12 Stela Berlin 14200 and statue Cairo CG589 (Porter and Moss 1934: 59; Moursi 1972: 52–56; 1987: 225–27; Borchardt 1911–1936: II, 144–45; Bryan 1991: 67–69).
13 E.g., Khaemwaset C and E as *sem*-Priest of Ptah under Rameses II and III (Khaemwaset C as high priest as well) and Meryatum B and Nebmaatre as high priests at Heliopolis under Rameses IV/V and IX.
14 Named daughters Iset C, Henuttaneb A, and S[it]amun are shown at Soleb (Porter and Moss 1952: 170[7]; Schiff Giorgini 1998–2003: V, pl. 97), with generic female children at Soleb (Schiff Giorgini 1998–2003: V, pl. 94, 127, 131) and in TT192 (Epigraphic Survey 1980: pl. 47, 57).
15 E.g., JE 33906, from Medinet Habu (Porter and Moss 1960–64: 774).
16 Cf. pp. 13–15.
17 Hayes 1951: fig. 27[KK].
18 In the mortuary temple of the pyramid at Meidum (Petrie 1892: pl. xxxvi[XVIII]: cf. Dodson 2009.

19 Classic statements in favor include (e.g.) Aldred 1959; 1968a: 100–16; 1988: 182; and Giles 2001: 25–137, with a rather different approach taken in Johnson 1996; the contrary case is put in (e.g.) Redford 1967: 88–169; Murnane 1977a: 123–69, 231–33; Gabolde 1998: 62–98.
20 Cf. Dorman 2008.
21 E.g., in the Soleb forehall and the gateway of its Pylon I (Schiff Giorgini 1998–2003: V, pl. 4–11, 20–23).
22 E.g., those shown in Forbes 1990.
23 Edinburgh NMS A.1956.347: see next note.
24 Cf. (conveniently) Aldred 1959: 19–24.
25 Although it was probably some time before it came into universal use — cf. Nims 1973.
26 Cf. Smith and Redford 1976; Redford 1988; Vergnieux and Gondran 1997.
27 Cf. Gohary 1992.
28 Murnane and van Siclen 1993.
29 The literature on Amarna is vast, but Kemp 1989: 261–317 (not in Kemp 2006) remains a key interpretation of Amarna as a community.
30 Cf. Ikram 1989.
31 And apparently the *ba*s of the deceased (Hornung 1999: 97).
32 Davies 1903–08; cf. Dodson and Ikram 2008: 229–32.
33 Martin 1974, 1989a; El-Khouly and Martin 1987; below, p. 18.
34 Fairman in Pendlebury 1951: 183.
35 Murnane and van Siclen 1993: 103–104.
36 TA1 and 2, for which see p. 27, below.
37 For which see Fairman in Pendlebury 1951: 153.
38 Cf. Fairman in Pendlebury 1951: 185.

Chapter 1: The Noonday Sun
1 Cf. Schulman 1982.
2 The inscription in TA2 is damaged, but the remains are fully consistent with the date being identical with that in TA1.
3 Cf. p. 6, above.
4 Durham 1964/188+1964/213+UPMAA E16022A-B, from Buhen (Smith 1976: 124–29, pl. xxix, lxxv); Darnell and Manassa 2007: 127 do, however, propose that the *durbar* was fundamentally a celebration of that Nubian campaign.
5 The figures are damaged, but no element of text has been lost.
6 Davies 1903–08: III, 5 n.5, *pace* ibid. I, 42.
7 Certainly after Year 5 when her mother first added "Neferneferuaten" to her name.
8 Thus also dating Ashmolean 1893.1, which shows the youngest of the five daughters apparently originally depicted on this fragmentary painted pavement (Davies 1921).
9 Nefertiti is shown alongside Amenhotep IV in the Amarna style in TT55, and so was certainly his wife before the Year 5/6 name change; she is also present in the Amenhotep-era *heb-sed* scenes at Karnak (Gohary 1992: 168). Given the important dualities behind king/queenship (cf. Troy 1986), it would seem

unlikely that the king would have long remained unwed after his accession (*pace* Gabolde 1998: 12–14).

10 See p. 139 n. 6, above.

11 Dodson 1991: 59–61.

12 See p. 139 n. 14, above.

13 Recently rediscovered in the Supreme Council of Antiquities store room there: see Hawass 2009.

14 Roeder 1969: pl. 105[56-VIII A], 106[831-VIII C]; Gabolde 2001: 26; 2002: 40; cf. Allen 2006: 7 n. 27 querying Gabolde's detection of a palimpsest text under the Tutankhuaten text.

15 An exception being Redford 1978–79, and much more recently Allen 2006: 16–17, the latter making him a son of Smenkhkare.

16 Budge proposed (1923: 1, half-heartedly seconded by Desroches-Noblecourt 1963: 133, 291) that his mother might have been a certain Meryetre, on the basis of a scarab from Abydos that linked a King's Mother of that name with a King Nebkheper*en*re, assuming a mistake for 'Nebkheper*u*re' — Tutankhaten's prenomen. However, he is more likely to be an obscure king of the Second Intermediate Period.

17 Harris 1974; Reeves 1988.

18 Quiring 1960; Manniche 1975; van Dijk 1997; Redford, 1984: 150, has also suggested Tadukhepa's aunt, Gilukhepa; cf. Helck 1984.

19 See p. 41, below.

20 For which dating, see pp. 27–31, below.

21 Hanke 1978: 190–91, fig. 57, on the basis of two largely erased texts on blocks 153/VIII and 442/VIIIA from Ashmunein (Roeder 1969: pl. 57, 11) that named a king's daughter (whose name is lost) directly ahead of Kiya's titles and name; for other potential depictions with a daughter, see Harris 1974: 30 n.6; cf. also p. 40, below. Others have made more ambitious claims for Kiya's later career, e.g., Perepelkin 1978: 108–30.

22 Cf. Robins 1991, 1992.

23 See pp. 95–98, below.

24 Cf. p. 25, below.

25 Cf. Merrillees 1987.

26 Amarna letter EA35 (Moran 1992: 107–19).

27 See p. 100, below.

28 Panagiotakopulu 2004.

29 Cf. Kozloff 2006 on the possibility of a previous outbreak under Amenhotep III.

30 Although rooms designed as store chambers were not infrequently used to hold the mummies of prematurely deceased royal family members (cf. Dodson 2003b).

31 That these were part of the basic plan, rather than an afterthought, is suggested by various geometric features of the tomb plan (see Lehner in Martin 1989a: 6).

32 Dodson and Ikram 2008: 224–28.

33 Cf. Martin 1989a: 47–48.

34 Gabolde 1998: 118–21; it should be noted that on the historical reconstruction adopted in the present book, Tutankhuaten will have been four or five at the time of Meketaten's death — hardly the nurseling shown (cf. p. 17, above).

35 Including Geoffrey Martin in his publication of the tomb (1989a: 43–45).

36 Davies 1903–08: V, 24–25.

37 In view of the presence of Nefertiti in the scenes: cf. pp. 37–40, below.

38 On the issue of children potentially borne by Meketaten's sisters, see p. 40, below.

39 Martin 1989a: 38–40 prefers to view them as two elements of a narrative, and reads considerable detail into the images, in spite of the fact that no trace of any label-texts survive.

40 Cf. also Arnold 1996: 115.

41 van Dijk 2006.

42 It may be noted that on the end of her sarcophagus Tiye is shown in a shrine receiving offerings from Akhenaten, Nefertiti, and Meryetaten (Brock 1996: 15, fig. 4, 17; Gabolde 1998: pl. xviiia), and apparently on wall E of the main burial chamber of the royal tomb (Martin 1989a: 23–24, pl. 25).

43 Martin 1989a: 47–48.

44 Cf. the continued use of shabtis, in some cases with a partly-Atenised version of the old chapter 6 of the Book of the Dead, in some with a version of the traditional *ḥtp-di-nsw* offering formula, and others (including those of the king) simply bearing the name and title of the owner: see Martin 1986.

45 Raven 1994: 7–8; Brock 1999: 11, 16; Gabolde 1998: 132–34, pl. xvi–xvii. It should be noted that most of the fragments attributed to Meketaten's sarcophagus by Martin 1974: 28–30 (and earlier scholars) are actually from the sarcophagus of Tiye: see further just below.

46 Cf. Gabolde 1998: 132–33.

47 Gabolde 1998: 136–37.

48 Martin 1989a: pl. 34.

49 Martin 1989a: pl. 36.

50 Martin 1989a: 31.

51 Martin 1989a: pl. 47, 48.

52 Martin 1989a: 34.

53 The presence of an amphora handle of Neferneferure in the southern branch of the Amarna Royal Wadi has been used to suggest her burial in a tomb there, but her youth and the interment of her sister in room γ might suggest room α—or possibly the intervening, but undecorated, room β—as a more likely venue.

54 Gabolde suggests that Setepenre might be the other interment in the room.

55 Lehner in Martin 1989a: 7–8, pl. 12a; this assumes the current burial chamber to be the "target," but a stairway in the center of this room could have continued the conceit deeper into the mountain.

56 Cf. Martin 1989a: 21.

57 Martin 1989a: 24.

58 Raven 1994; Brock 1999; Gabolde 1998: 134–36, pl. xviii–xxia.

59 Cf. Gabolde 1998: pl. xxib.

60 See pp. 41, 47, below.

61 For which see Gabolde 1998: 139–40.

62 Cf. p. 131.

63 Cf. Krauss 1978: 99–100; Raven 1994: 18.

64 For the further possibility that they represent a later reburial of Tiye's mummy, see below, p. 76.

65 Cf. Davies 1903–08: III, 4. Or simply because she was Huya's direct employer!

66 Davies 1903–08: III, pl. iv, vi, viii, ix, xviii; the manufacture of a statue of her is also shown: ibid, pl. xvii, xviii.

67 Apart from a mention of an estate of hers on a jar docket from Amarna (Pendlebury 1951: 164), there were also estates in the name of Amenhotep III and Tiye, as well as most of the other members of Akhenaten's family.

68 Especially as she appears in Amenhotep III's half of the lintel in the tomb that balances Akhenaten, Nefertiti, and their daughters with Amenhotep III, Tiye, and Baketaten on the other (Davies 1903–08: III, pl. xviii).

69 Porter and Moss 1960–64: 128; cf. Dodson 1990: 89.

70 Nevertheless, Gabolde has proposed (1992) that she was actually the now-nameless daughter of Kiya depicted with her mother at Ashmunein (cf. p. 141 n. 21, above).

Chapter 2: The Waning Sun

1 Cf. Davies 1903–08: II, 6–8, although recognizing that considerations of space and design may well have played a role in the number of princesses chosen for depiction.

2 The cartouches were cut from the wall in the 1880s, surviving only in early travelers' copies (Newberry 1928: 5–6; Mosley 2009: 138, 142–43), including a squeeze made by Carl Richard Lepsius and now in Berlin (Mosely 2009: 144–45). The king's nomen was even then damaged, but its true reading seems difficult to doubt (although Mosely [2009: 144–50] argues that the cartouche is actually a partly erased nomen of Akhenaten. This is wholly untenable on the basis of the very squeeze that she herself publishes).

3 See pp. 35–36, below; cf. Montserrat 2000: 168–73.

4 Cairo JE62172.

5 Loeben 1991, 1994. A very similar jar found with it, JE62176, also had its inscription erased, but the traces are now wholly illegible.

6 Witness the Amenhotep III/Akhenaten debate: cf. p. 6, above.

7 Shaw 1984; Shannon 1987; Pendlebury 1951: 75, pl. c[22, 23, 24]; Kemp 2008/9: 45; cf. n. 29, just below, on issues surrounding the reporting of objects bearing Smenkhkare's name.

8 Pendlebury 1951: 194.

9 Pendlebury 1951: 60.

10 Pendlebury 1951: 75, 80.

11 Pendlebury 1951: 150, 194, pl. lxxxii[III].

12 Traunecker and Traunecker 1984–85.

13 Cf. p. 45, below.

14 Pendlebury 1951: pl. lxxxvi, xcviii[35]; cf. 199.

15 Porter and Moss 1974–81: 839. A further lost block once thought to include a depiction of Smenkhkare walking behind Akhenaten has now been shown to be a product of overenthusiastic modern graphical restoration (Málek 1996).

16 Hayes 1951: 232–33, fig. 34[R20].

17 Which, as in TA2, omits the feminine *t*-ending.

18 Cairo JE 62654 (Beinlich and Saleh 1989: 20[46*gg*]).

19 Cairo JE62662 (Beinlich and Saleh 1989: 38[101s]).

20 On the Sheikh Abd el-Qurna hill, and dating to the reign of Amenhotep III.

21 See pp. 34, 44–46, below.

22 Cf. Chapters 3 and 5, below.

23 Petrie 1890: pl. xxiii; 1894: pl. xv.

24 Specifically Thutmose I, III, and IV, together with Amenhotep III (von Beckerath 1999: 135–43). Interestingly, however, Akhenaten consistently used an extended prenomen: there are no known examples of his ever having used the simple form "Neferkheperure" to refer to himself.

25 Cairo JE61500a; Beinlich and Saleh 1989: 4[1k].

26 Porter and Moss 1960–64: 253[5]).

27 See Newberry 1928.

28 Cf. Murnane 1977a: 169–79.

29 Thus the name "Smenkhkare" was used when reporting any material that used either of the prenomina and nomina. When evaluating data from the pre-1980s excavations this can cause major problems. For example, Pendlebury 1951: 74 lists the discovery of two "Smenkhkarē'" faience rings at Amarna: checking the Type-codes indicates that while one indeed refers to Smenkhkare (reading "Ankhkheperure"), the other actually reads "Ankhkheperure-mery-Waenre"— the prenomen invariably found with the nomen "Neferneferuaten." Verifying the actual reading is not straightforward, as the Types in question are not illustrated in any of the volumes that publish the work of the Egypt Exploration Society at Amarna between the two World Wars. Rather, they appear only in Petrie 1894, but under completely different reference numbers, which can only be cross-referred by consulting one of the appendices of Frankfort and Pendlebury 1933!

30 Harris 1973a; 1973b; 1974; 1977.

31 Cairo JE60714 (Porter and Moss 1960–64: 575); for earlier debate as to its gender, cf. Vandersleyen 1992: 75–76. On its general proportions, cf. pp. 78–79, below.

32 Cf. Newberry 1928: 7; Montserrat 2000: 168–73.

33 In favor, adding further to Harris's arguments, e.g., Samson 1973, 1976, 1977, 1978, 1979, 1982z–d, 1985; Reeves 2001: 167–79; against, e.g., Aldred 1968a; 1988; Giles 1970; Tawfik 1975; Loeben 1986; Dodson 1981, 1992a, 1993b, 1994b, 2001, 2002a, 2003a, and 2005a.

34 Thus following in the footsteps of Sobkneferu and Hatshepsut.

35 See pp. 40–42, below.

36 Krauss 1978: 43–47.

37 Including the present writer until as late as 2002–2003.

38 Gabolde 1998: 153–57.

39 Allen 2006; Gabolde 2008.

40 Cf. p. 50, below.

41 See appendix 3 for all known variants of Neferneferuaten's cartouches.

42 Cf. Perepelkin 1978: 85–130.

43 MFA 64.521 (Freed, Markowitz and D'Auria 1999: 238[110–13]).

44 Krauss 1978; Gabolde 1998.

45 Allen 2006.

46 The only "evidence" cited by Allen (2006: 15 n.63) for a marriage is what seems to be a corrupt label text in the tomb-chapel of Meryre i (TA4), where a ♡-sign has been substituted for the ⌂-sign seen in all other label texts on this section of wall (Davies 1903–08: pl. xix; cf. Robins 1981: 75–76). Allen in any case admits these are far earlier than the marriage between Akhenaten and Nefer-neferuaten-tasherit that he posits for Year 16/17. It is also worth pointing out that in the Year 12 scenes in TA2, Neferneferuaten-tasherit is unequivocally a simple princess.

47 Louvre AF9904 + Brooklyn 33.51 (Loeben 1986, 1999; cf. Buvot 1999 and Allen 2006: 14).

48 Amarna Letters EA10 and 11.

49 Amarna Letter EA155; Gabolde uses this letter to support his view that Meryetaten had actually become coregent with Akhenaten (1998: 174–78).

50 For a novel suggestion that is not, however, compatible with the chronological scheme adopted here, see p. 149 n. 18, below.

51 Cf. Murnane 1977a.

52 Cf. Giles 2001: 255–69; Grajetzki 2006: 33–34.

53 See pp. 40–42, below.

54 Harrison 1966; Harrison, Connolly, and Abdalla 1969.

55 E.g., Roeder 1969: pl. 18[340-VIA, 652-VIIIA], 127[783-VIII], 159[364-VIII].

56 Roeder 1969: pl. 106[451-VIIC]; cf. Gabolde 1998: 121–22 n. 997.

57 Redford 1975: 11–12, pl. vii; note that the restoration provided there is pure speculation, as we have no idea of the context of this isolated block on the original wall.

58 Helck 1984: 21.

59 See pp. 18–23, above.

60 With the wife being of (just about) mature age!

61 For bibliography see Grimm and Schoske (eds.) 2001, with summaries of the various published theories on pp. 121–36; to this add in particular Gabolde 2008. The contents of the tomb are usefully summarized in Bell 1990.

62 See p. 145 n. 70, below.

63 Filer 2000; Germer 2001; but cf. the concerns about the aging of premodern remains raised by Molleson and Cox 1993: 167–79.

64 On the other hand, Gabolde (2008: 16) argues that the early depictions of Amenhotep IV in TT55 (Porter and Moss 1960–64: 109[7]) and on Berlin 2072 (our fig. 5) are those of a nine- to ten-year-old boy, thus allowing the KV55 body to be his. However, the aspects of the reliefs which he posits as diagnostic of a child are just those features seen in the post-jubilee images of Amenhotep III, which one would have expected to have carried over into his son's reign.

65 Yoshimura and Kondo 1995: 18.

66 For which see pp. 52, 61, below.

67 Harrison 1966: 114–15, pl. xxviii; curiously, the author uses a photograph of the face of the middle coffin to demonstrate the facial similarity between the KV55 mummy and Tutankhamun.

68 See p. 44 and p. 152 n. 120, below.

69 Cf. below on Akhenaten's increasing religious intolerance.

70 The modifications carried out are detailed by Allen 1988: 122–26 and Gabolde 1998: 237–55, pl. xxx–xxxvi; Allen withdrew his conclusions in his 2006 paper in light of Grimm 2001, but neither the present writer nor Marc Gabolde (personal communication November 6, 2008, and implicitly in Gabolde 2008) finds Grimm's arguments convincing.

71 Part now Petrie Museum UC410, part now Cairo JE 64959 (Stewart 1975: 22, pl. 12, 52.2).

72 Allen 1988: 117–21, albeit with rather different conclusions; cf. also Gabolde 1998: 162–66, pl. xxiv.

73 In spite of Gabolde 1998: pl. xxiv.

74 Weatherhead 2007: 257–9[12.1] (now Liverpool 1973.1.545A[PP]), 258, 260[12.12]).

75 Peet and Wooley 1923: 8, fig. 1; Kemp 2004: 16–17, fig. 2.

76 Porter and Moss 1960–64: 252–54; Kampp 1996: I, 426–27.

77 The flourish below the *mr*-sign is surely a feminine *t*.

78 All we have are apparently discrepant death/accession dates, e.g., as regards Thutmose III and Amenhotep II (Redford 1965).

79 Pendlebury 1951: pl. xcv[279].

80 Hoffmeier and Abd el-Maksoud 2003: 180–81, figs. 7–8; Hoffmeier 2006: 262, 276 fig. 23; Ertman and Hoffmeier 2007: 39.

81 Ertman and Hoffmeier 2007, 2008, who prefer "one of the individuals with the throne name Ankhkheperure" (2008: 301–302), although there is no sign of Smenkhkare at the site.

82 For the Temple of Nebkheperure, see pp. 67–68, below.

83 Gardiner 1928.

84 See Gardiner 1928: pl. v, top.

85 Kansas City, Nelson-Atkins Museum 67–21/5–6; NMS A.1959.451 (Harris 1974: 15, 17 fig. 3; 1992: 60).

86 Bickel 1997: 92–94.

87 It should be noted, however, that her evidence, from a gateway of Amenhotep III's memorial temple, concerns Amun's figure being replaced by that of Amenhotep III, rather than the erasure without recarving that is characteristic of the persecution.

88 For whom, see pp. 98, 114, below.

89 Mut's name is still intact in one scene in TA25 (Ay—Davies 1903–08: VI, pl. xxvi) and two in TA14 (May—Davies 1903–08: V, pl. iii, v), while it has been erased in TA7 (Parennefer—Davies 1903–08: VI, 4, pl. iv); in TA6 (Panehsy—Davies 1903–08: II, pl. v, viii), TA8 (Tutu—Davies 1903–08: VI, 10, pl. xvi) and TA20 (anonymous—Davies 1903–08: V, pl. xv) Mutnodjmet's name and titles have been largely destroyed, leaving the status of the Mut-vulture unknown in these cases.

90 Davis 1910: 14; unfortunately this section of the text is only available in hieroglyphic type, no extant drawing or photograph allowing it to be verified.

91 Cf. Raven 1994: 19.

92 Although Maat's name came to be spelled out, avoiding the use of her ideogram.

93 See pp. 62–65, above.

94 There is also a rather unexpected attack on fecundity figures, the portly offering-bearing genii, in certain contexts (Eaton-Krauss 1988: 10).

95 Aldred 1968a: 246.

96 The "u" was apparently dropped on his accession.

97 See pp. 90–92, below.

98 Not to mention the fact that hardly anything of the interior surfaces actually survives today: cf. Martin 1974: 31–32.

99 Cairo JE62028 (Eaton-Krauss 2008: 25–56[1]). There has been considerable debate as to whether this might originally have been made for another king (cf. Vandersleyen 1984–85: 320; 1992: 77, followed by others: see Eaton-Krauss 2008: 42 n.98), but the stylistic points involved are highly subjective and the alterations visible may well have been carried out when updating the names of the king and queen (see Eaton-Krauss 2008: 42–45).

100 Cairo JE62030; the Amun form of the king's name has been substituted in one place only (Eaton-Krauss 2008: 75–91[4]).

101 Berlin 14197 (Porter and Moss 1934: 232), partly destroyed (including the king's figure) during World War II.

102 Ockinga 1997.

103 Cf. p. 101, below, for potential further links with the royal family.

104 Zivie 1998; 2007: 72–75.

105 Cf. Dodson 1990: 89.

106 Shannon 1987.

107 Pendlebury 1951: 159–60.

108 Cf. Kemp 1987: 44–49.

109 El-Khouly and Martin 1987; cf. p. 42, above, for TA28.

110 Cairo JE60688–91 (Porter and Moss 1960–64: 574; Beinlich and Saleh 1989: 106–17[266g]; Dodson (forthcoming) a; I now withdraw unreservedly the conclusions reached in Dodson 2002a and 2003a).

111 Cairo JE60673 (Beinlich and Saleh 1989: 83, 85–88[256a-b]; Dodson (forthcoming) a).

112 Cairo JE61517, 61902a (Porter and Moss 1960–64: 581; McLeod 1970: 10–12, pl. 17, 20; Beinlich and Saleh 1989: 22[h]).

113 Cairo JE61495 (Porter and Moss 1960–64: 579; Beinlich and Saleh 1989: 31–32[79]).

114 Cairo JE62416 (Porter and Moss 1960–64: 583; Beinlich and Saleh 1989: 222[620[41–42]).

115 Cairo JE61944 (Beinlich and Saleh 1989: 96[261p(1)]; Gabolde 2008: 17–19).

116 Cf. Harris 1992: 59–62, to be corrected and enlarged in a forthcoming work by Marc Gabolde.

117 Eaton-Krauss 1993: 9–23.

118 The idea that Neferneferuaten's tomb was entered at the time of Tutankhamun's death and stripped to make up shortages in his own outfit (cf. Fairman 1961: 39) is highly unlikely.

Chapter 3: The Northern Problem

1 Cf. Cohen and Westbrook 2000; Bryce 2003; Darnell and Manassa 2007: 149–52.
2 Cf. Darnell and Manassa 2007: 137–47, 153–61.
3 Battle reliefs from Karnak once attributed to Akhenaten actually belong to Tutankhamun (Johnson 1992: 38–39).
4 Gabolde 1998: 195–207; Darnell and Manassa 2007: 172–76.
5 Moran 1992. Each letter is referred to by a serial number, prefixed in the following notes with 'EA'—not to be confused with the 'EA' prefix used in the museum numbers of Egyptian antiquites in the British Museum: all the latter numbers are given in this book as 'BM EA.'
6 Güterbock 1956.
7 Murnane 1990 is a key source for discussions of matters concerning Egypto-Hittite relations during the latter part of the Eighteenth Dynasty; cf. also Kitchen 1962 and Spalinger 1979.
8 EA17.
9 Also referred to as the SA.GAZ.
10 EA157.
11 EA41.
12 See p. 64, below.
13 Martin 1989b; Schneider 1996; Strouhal 2008; Aston and Bourriau (in preparation); Raven (forthcoming).
14 Martin 1989b: 87–92, pl. 99–108.
15 Martin 1989b: 94–97, pl. 110a–117.
16 See p. 68, below.
17 Cairo JE61467 (Porter and Moss 1960–64: 577–78).
18 See p. 68, below.
19 Cf. Darnell and Manassa 2007: 178–82.
20 *Deeds of Shuppiliumash*, frag. 28.

Chapter 4: The Living Image of Amun

1 Cf. Eaton-Krauss 1987.
2 Cairo CG34183; Porter and Moss 1972: 52–53.
3 Cairo CG34184; Porter and Moss 1972: 10.
4 Although later usurped by Horemheb, the name was clearly originally Tutankhamun, rather than Tutankhaten (Harris 1973c).
5 Cf. p. 115, below.
6 Bennett 1939.
7 Cf. also below, pp. 119–20, for similar documents under Horemheb.
8 Gardiner 1947: I, 14*–19*; for the wider potential meaning of the title by the late Eighteenth Dynasty, see pp. 101–102, below.
9 Wine-jar dockets found in Horemheb's private tomb: (Schneider 1996: 12[25a–b, 27a–b]).
10 Listed in full by Martin 1989b: 163–64.
11 Paramessu, later Rameses I, held a very similar title during the last years of Horemheb: cf. p. 128, below.
12 Cf. Gardiner 1953a: 10–11; cf. 1947: I, 16*–19*.

13 Although many of Horemheb's titles are known only from his tomb; Ay's Tutankhamun-era sepulcher has never been identified.
14 See pp. 90–99, below.
15 Reeves 1981; cf. p. 108, below.
16 Cairo JE 57438; Porter and Moss 1960–64: 588.
17 Ockinga 1997: 35, pl. 38–39.
18 Gabolde 1987.
19 Sa'ad 1975; Eaton-Krauss 1988: 2–3; Schaden 1992: 101, 103.
20 Le Saout 1982a: 244–46.
21 It has even been proposed that the blocks could have been brought to Karnak from Thebes–West as were a number of blocks from Horemheb's memorial temple (cf. Johnson 1992: 45–46).
22 Schaden 1977: 153–91; Eaton-Krauss 1988: 4–11; Gabolde and Gabolde 1989; Johnson 1992: 22–25, 43–47.
23 As reconstructed by Marc Gabolde, who will be publishing the material in due course: see Johnson 1992: 22, 193 fig. 23.
24 Johnson 1992: 9–47.
25 Whence they seem to have been transported in medieval times, along with other ex-Akhenaten blocks reused by Horemheb and Rameses II.
26 Johnson 1992: 48–82.
27 Johnson 1992: 13, 165–68 [44–48]; Darnell and Manassa 2007: 120–22; see also Johnson 2009–2010.
28 Cf. p. 57, above.
29 Cf. Darnell and Manassa 2007: 127–31.
30 Eaton-Krauss and Murnane 1991: 31–34.
31 Forbes 2000.
32 Brand 1999; 2000: 45–118.
33 Murnane 1979.
34 Epigraphic Survey 1994, 1998.
35 Epigraphic Survey 1998: xvii.
36 Epigraphic Survey 1994: xix–xx.
37 Hayes 1951: 177, 239; fig. 33[S125], 34[R21], 37; cf. van Dijk and Eaton-Krauss 1986: 33 n. 8.
38 Schiff Giorgini 1965, 1998–2003.
39 BM EA2.
40 BM EA1–2 (Porter and Moss 1952: 212).
41 But not installed: see p. 104, below.
42 Although it could be a reference to Amenhotep as simply a male ancestor.
43 Chicago OI 12144 (Larson 1992; one could, however, read the hieroglyphs as making him Tutankhamun's great-grandfather—or simply an indeterminate "forefather": cf. Reeves 1982).
44 Macadam 1955: 12–14, 28–44. Given that the site's ancient name was Gem(pa)aten, it is likely that it had originally been built by Amenhotep III, one of whose scarabs and a statue base were found nearby.
45 Bell 1985.
46 Porter and Moss 1952: 124.

47 Davies and Gardiner 1926.

48 Cf. Darnell and Manassa 2007: 127–31.

49 Darnell 2003; Darnell and Manassa 2007: 113–37.

50 Cf. van Dijk and Eaton-Krauss 1986.

51 Porter and Moss 1974–81: 334.

52 Cairo JE88131 (Habachi 1979: 34–35).

53 Berlin (Habachi 1979: 32–35).

54 Petrie Museum UC14470 (Stewart 1976: 50–51, pl. 41).

55 Porter and Moss 1974–81: 414.

56 Porter and Moss 1974–81: 781; Dodson 1999: 62; 2005: 76.

57 Châaban 1919: 205–206.

58 Cairo JE 57195.

59 van Dijk and Eaton-Krauss 1986.

60 Petrie Museum UC23806 (Petrie 1894: pl. xv[117]); UC1927 (Samson in Pendlebury 1951: 230, pl. cviii).

61 See p. 123, below.

62 Unfortunately the Tutankhamun seal impressions found in KV55 bear only his prenomen (Reeves 1990a: 44, pl. ii[8, 10, 12–14]).

63 Cf. pp. 40–41, above.

64 Tiye could at this point have been moved to WV22 if her mummy had ever been in KV55.

65 Broadly as proposed by Aldred 1968a: 140–62; the author withdraws his previous proposals on the history of the deposit (published in Dodson 1992a; 1993b; 1994a: 57–61; 1994b; 2001; 2002a; 2003a; and 2003b).

66 E.g., Aldred 1968a: 154; Reeves 1990a: 44–49.

67 Cross 2008, 2009.

68 Cf. Cross 2008: 308–10; 2009: 18.

69 Cf. Murnane 1977b: 307–308 on the question of whether the remains of a mummy apparently found in the 1890s might have belonged to any of TA26's original occupants.

70 <http://www.nicholasreeves.com/item.aspx?category=Comment&id=81>.

71 For a basic list of statues from Karnak, see Reeves 1990b: 27; for Luxor, see Johnson 1994.

72 Cf. Brand 1999.

73 Robins 1994: 148–59.

74 Cairo JE60714: cf. p. 35, above.

75 Cairo JE60715 (unpublished).

76 Robins 1984; 1994: 148–50, without the distinction of ownership (or gender: cf. Vandersleyen 1992: 75–76).

77 Cf. Chapter 8, below.

78 Berlin 12411: Porter and Moss 1974–81: 711–12; Schulman 1965; Maystre 1977; but see further below, pp. 101–102 for the alternative that the figure is that of another senior soldier, Nakhtmin B.

79 Cairo TR 22/6/37/1 (Habachi 1979: 36).

80 TT31 (Khonsu-To) and TT324 (Hatiay), dating to the reign of Rameses II (Porter and Moss 1960–64: 47–49, 395–96; Habachi 1979: 36–37; Ockinga 1994).

81 Habachi 1979: 37–39.
82 Habachi 1979: 39.
83 Interestingly, the epithet "Doer of Maat" is one used by Ay when king: cf. p. 99, below.
84 Habachi 1979: 35–36.
85 Van Dijk 1990.
86 Cairo JE60720, 60826.
87 See pp. 120, 128, below.
88 Liverpool University E.583 (Amer 1985).
89 Cf. p. 95, below; May's figure and name were erased in this chapel (Davies 1903–08: V, 2–3, pl. ii, iv, xix), presumably as a result of his falling out of Akhenaten's favor, although van Dijk (1990: 26) suggests that Maya could have erased them himself, to blot out traces of his past.
90 Copenhagen ÆIN102 (Porter and Moss 1999: 681[801–655–570]).
91 Hayes 1951: 101 n. 27.
92 Raven 2005: 1–6.
93 Cairo CG 34186 (Porter and Moss 1974–81: 870).
94 Fitzwilliam E.SS.54 (Bourriau 1988; Martin 2005: 61–62).
95 Porter and Moss 1960–64: 75–78; Habachi 1980: 633.
96 Khartoum 2680: Macadam 1955: 1–3, pl. 2–3[1].
97 Simpson 1963: 2–18, pl. iii–ix.
98 Cf. Bierbrier 1977: 1243.
99 For his monuments, see Maystre 1992: 279–80[72–75].
100 Raven 2002; Raven, van Walsem, et al. (in preparation); he may also in the interim have built a tomb (TA4) at Amarna, but the identity of the Saqqara and Amarna Meryres remains a moot point.
101 Martin 1991a; Horemheb: Martin 1989b; Schneider 1996; Aston and Bourriau (in preparation); Strouhal 2008; Maya: van Dijk et al. (in preparation); Raven et al. 2001; Aston and Aston (in preparation).
102 Most notably the tomb of Rameses II's sister and brother-in-law (Martin 1997) and the vizier Neferrenpet (Saqqara ST0: Tawfik 1991).
103 Firth and Gunn 1926; Quibell and Hayter 1927.
104 Zivie 2000; 2007.
105 Hasegawa 2003.
106 van Dijk 1988.
107 Cf. the tombs of the vizier Aperel (I.1) and the Chief Outline Draftsman Thutmose (I.19) on the Saqqara escarpment (Zivie 1990; 2007: 26–51, 66–71) and the dating of the first stage of Meryneith's tomb to the earlier years of Akhenaten.
108 Schulman 1964b; Spalinger 1982; 2005.
109 Cf. Schulman 1964a.
110 Cf. p. 57, above.
111 Cairo JE60837, 60827–8, 60830, 60836–7.
112 See p. 99, below.
113 Cf. Kemp 1987: 44–49.
114 Schaden 1979.
115 Drenkhahn 1983.

116 Cairo JE59905–60133 (Hölscher 1939: 85–98, pl. 52–56).

117 Cairo JE59896; Chicago OI 41088 (Porter and Moss 1972: 458–59); it should be noted that these were originally inscribed for Ay, and only the features suggest Tutankhamun.

118 Robichon and Varille 1936: I, 29, 41–42, pl. iv[3], xii, xiii, xix, xxxvi–xxxviii[1] (North Temple); 47, pl. iv[4], xvi–xix, xli, xlii[1] (South Temple).

119 Robichon and Varille 1938: 99–100.

120 Given the similarity between the plans of the two temples, it is possible that if one is that of Tutankhamun, the other could be that of Rameses I—or even the lost temple of Smenkhkare (cf. p. 40, above)? See p. 149 n. 21, above, for the suggestion that the temple was demolished and the blocks reused at Karnak.

121 Cf. Tawfik 1994 for a dissenting voice.

122 The vizier Amenemopet (TT29) was buried in KV48, and the absence of a sub-structure from the tomb-chapel of Rekhmire (TT100) suggests similar arrangements were planned for him.

123 Yuya and Tjuiu doubtless had a now lost chapel in the Sheikh Abd el-Qurna/Asasif area like many of their contemporaries.

124 Cross 2008: 309, fig. 5.

125 Romer 1981: 169.

126 Cf. eg., the 273/274-day gap between the death of Meresankh III and her burial (Dunham and Simpson 1974: 8).

127 Discovered in 2005 (see www.kv-63.com), the fact that the deposit was sealed by the same flood that covered KV62, probably during the reign of Ay (see p. 76) makes it difficult to attribute its contents to any other king: the form of the coffins used as storage containers in KV63 makes it clear that they cannot date prior to the reign of Amenhotep III, who was buried in the West Valley and thus unlikely to have been KV63's owner. The long known but modestly sized embalming cache of Tutankhamun in KV54 (Porter and Moss 1960–64: 586) would thus be a supplementary deposit, perhaps of items accidentally overlooked when KV63 was closed.

128 Leek 1972: 19–20.

129 E.g., Brier 1998 cf. Reeves 2001: 187–89.

130 Cf. the review in Counsell 2008; the 1968 and 2005 examinations are both still without formal publication, and thus one is reliant on informal summaries in various online and printed contexts, including <http://guardians.net/hawass/press_release_tutankhamun_ct_scan_results.htm> and Hawass 2005: 263–70.

131 E.g., those from the tombs of Thutmose III, Amenhotep II, Horemheb, and Rameses I/Sethy I.

132 Carter and Mace 1923–33: II, 196.

Chapter 5: The Zananzash Affair

1 See Bryce 1990 and Murnane 1990: 22–31 for the major issues and interpretations of this episode.

2 Cf. Kitchen 1985: 44.

3 Although Harris, as reported by Reeves 2001: 176–77, has implicitly no problem with this.

4 Helck 1984; cf. p. 41, above.

5 Cf. Bryce 1990: 104–105.

6 See p. 88.

7 Cf. Kitchen 1995: 333 n. 498.

8 El-Khouli, Holthoer, Hope, and Kaper 1993: 147–52; cf. Cross 2009: 16–18 and p. 158 n. 51, below..

9 Possibly painted after the closure of the sarcophagus: the paintings on the opposite wall must have been done after the shrines around the sarcophagus were in place, as they cover the false wall between the antechamber and the burial chamber, which can only have been built at this point. On decoration being applied after a royal burial, cf. Romer 1975: 330, 341, showing that the Amduat was applied to the walls of Thutmose III's burial chamber subsequent to the sealing of its side chambers.

10 El-Khouli, Holthoer, Hope, and Kaper 1993: 164.

11 Cf. Murnane 1990: 132–36.

12 Dziobek 1992: 48, 52, 54.

13 Wilkinson 2000: 92. On the other hand, Ramesside data shows the new king's Year 1 being counted from the moment of the old king's death (e.g., Kitchen 1968–90: IV, 382, for the transition from Sethy II to Siptah).

14 Cf. Dodson and Hilton 2004: 15–16; as noted in p. 139 n. 18, above, it is possible that the formal nomination of Amenhotep E/IV is mentioned in a Meidum graffito.

15 Cf. Hatshepsut as regent for Thutmose III, and later Tawosret for Siptah.

16 *Deeds*, frag. 31.

17 Cf. p. 100, below.

18 It should be noted that Gabolde has proposed that Zananzash did actually reach Egypt—and became King Smenkhkare before his demise (1998: 187–226). On the view taken in this book that Smenkhkare's reign was wholly contained within that of Akhenaten, this reconstruction is wholly impossible.

19 On the other hand, some degree of power struggle between Ay and Horemheb during the interregnum is not improbable: cf. van Dijk 1996.

20 E.g., KV17 (Hornung 1991: pl. 99–106, 114–24).

Chapter 6: God's Father to God

1 Cf. p. 80, above.

2 Cf. Schulman 1964b: 46–47.

3 Berlin 17555, bought in Akhmim (Roeder 1924: II, 267–68; Kaiser (ed.) 1967: 56[583]).

4 Formerly in the Omar Pasha Sultan collection (Martin 1986: 118–19[15]); it was sold (for $189,000) at Sotheby's in New York on December 17, 1997 (from the Barratt Brown Collection), and then re-sold at Bonhams for £215,650 on July 14, 2004. Martin also attributes MMA 45.4.7 and another Omar Pasha Sultan piece to Ay (1986: 118[13–14]), but although both belong to a God's Father whose name contains the same radicals as that of Ay, the orthographies of the names differ from Ay's invariable 𓉭𓏤𓏤 reading respectively 𓈖𓏤 and 𓐍𓏤.

5 Pendlebury 1951: pl. xcii[196–97], xciv[253]. 0

6 See Jones 2000: 345[1283].

7 Habachi 1958.

8 Ryholt 1997: 222–31.

9 Ockinga 1997: 55–56, *pace* Brunner 1961 and Bryan 1991: 44–46; cf. further
   below p. 101, below.

10 See n. 4, just above, end: they might even, following Martin, actually belong to Ay.

11 E.g., Noble (*iry-pʿt*), Count (*ḥȝty-ʿ*), Sole Companion (*smr-wʿty*), Royal Seal
   Bearer (*ḥtmty-bity*).

12 Davis 1907: xiv–xv.

13 E.g., in particular Aldred 1957.

14 See p. 99, below.

15 Cf. n. 13, just above. Aldred further posited that the owner of shabti MMA
   45.4.7 might actually have been both Yuya's father and predecessor in office.

16 Brock 1999.

17 Cf. Birrell 1997.

18 Davis 1907: xvi–xvii.

19 Cf. p. 101, below.

20 Cf. Schaden 1992: 94–98.

21 E.g., Schaden 1977: 162, 164, 166; 1992: 102, bottom.

22 Cf. Schaden 1992: 105–106.

23 TA6 (Panehsy—Davies 1903–08: II, pl. v, viii), TA7 (Parennefer—Davies
   1903–08: VI, 4, pl. iv), TA8 (Tutu: Davies 1903–08: VI, 10, pl. xvi), TA14
   (May—Davies 1903–08: V, pl. iii, v), TA20 (anonymous—Davies 1903–08: V,
   pl. xv) and TA25 (Ay himself—Davies 1903–08: VI, pl. xxvi).

24 Cf. Sethe 1905: 135; Davies 1903–08: 18 n.1; Helck 1973: 251–53; Hari 1976.

25 Cf. Aldred 1968a: 105–106.

26 Cairo CG779 (Porter and Moss 1960–64: 784–85).

27 E.g., Schulman 1964a: 62–63.

28 E.g., Habachi 1980: 633, 638 n.86; Morkot 1985.

29 See p. 108, below.

30 Cairo JE35626, apparently from Sheikh Abd el-Qurna (Helck 1955–58: 1908–1909).

31 Van Dijk 1993: 60–61 uses the name of Nakhtmin's mother to suggest that he could
   rather have been only a grandson of Ay, on the grounds that no other wife than Tey
   was known. However, if Iuy had died prior to the building of Ay's Amarna tomb
   there would be no obvious context in which to find her, particularly given the incomplete state of the tomb and the royal-family-centricity of Amarna tomb-chapel décor.

32 There seems no reason, as proposed by Schulman 1964c: 125, to equate Nakhtmin
   with the General Nakht of roughly the same period, who owned the Books of
   the Dead BM EA10471 and 10473 (Glanville 1927).

33 There are a few examples of a simple form without any epithet, and a few
   scarabs with the alternate epithet "beloved of Amun."

34 A few examples lack the final epithet—but all have "God's Father."

35 As such, he only seems to have usurped one monument from Tutankhamun, a
   statue of Amun (Chicago OI 10503 [Johnson 1992: 24 n.99; Malek 1999: 1025]).

36 *KUB* XIX 20: see Murnane 1990: 25–28.

37 Laroche 1971 378.2.

38 Berlin 1920/73 (34316) (Krauss and Ullrich 1982).

39 Ockinga 1997: 55–56.

40 BMA 67.174.1 (James 1974: 172[25]); it is not impossible, however, that the queen referred to might rather be Tiye A, wife of Amenhotep III, on the basis of the effectively identical hieroglyphic spellings of the two queens' names. However, taking into account the dating of the statue, it seems most likely that Ay B's aunt was the contemporary queen, i.e., Tey—unless the Ay cartouche is actually secondary (cf. Freed, Markowitz, and D'Auria (eds.) 1999: 279).

41 See p. 79, above.

42 Cf. Gardiner 1953a: 9–10.

43 Cf. van Dijk 1993: 59–63.

44 Porter and Moss 1952: 122; Černý and Edel [1963]a.

45 His son Amenemopet, shown with Paser in his shrine, later became viceroy himself, after the intervening viceroyalty of Iuni (Habachi 1980: 633–34).

46 Habachi and Anus 1977: 16, fig. 8–9, pl. iiia, iva; Ay's name appears in the chapel of the tomb's pyramid, which Porter and Moss 1960–64: 350 mistakenly refer to as the tomb's "burial chamber."

47 Habachi and Anus 1977: 28–30.

48 Cf. Habachi and Anus 1977: pl. iva.

49 Porter and Moss 1960–64: 91–95; Pereyra De Fidanza 2000.

50 Cairo CG34187 (Porter and Moss 1974–81: 18); cf. also p. 157 n. 18 for an attempt to link a Mutnodjmet mentioned on the stela with the wife of Horemheb.

51 Louvre E.25429 (Vandier 1968).

52 Berlin 2074 and Louvre C55 (Porter and Moss 1937: 22).

53 Cf. pp. 79, 101, above.

54 Kuhlmann 1979; Klemm 1988: 48–49.

55 Porter and Moss 1937: 17; Kuhlmann 1979: 174, pl. 52b.

56 See below, p. 104.

57 Although Johnson prefers Ankhesenamun (1994: 148).

58 Davies 1933: 21, pl. ix, xii.

59 Davies 1903–08 VI, pl. xxv.

60 Louvre C56 (Pierret 1878: II, 44–47).

61 Edwards 1939: 6–9; cf. p. 71, above. Still later, both lions were removed to Gebel Barkal by the Nubian king Amunislo.

62 Now Berlin 19915 (Porter and Moss 1974–81: 334).

63 MFA 09.641 (Porter and Moss 1974–81: 831)

64 BM stela EA211 (Porter and Moss 1974–81: 742).

65 Cf. p. 67, above. Eaton-Krauss 1988: 11 n. 74 suggests that Ay may at this time have erased his representations as a commoner where they occurred in the earlier part of the temple, as not "in accordance with his altered status." However, this goes against normal New Kingdom practice, which was to leave pre-accession depictions alone, or at most add *uraei* to their foreheads (cf. Horemheb, Merenptah and Amenmeses [as the former Messuy]—p. 122, below). A unique variant is the addition of kingly cartouches (replacing those of his father?) to the end of the sash of Prince Rameses A (= Rameses II) in the Corridor of the Kings in Sethy I's Abydos Temple (Brand 2000: 318, fig. 82).

66 Cairo CG602+CG608+TR6/11/26/8 (Porter and Moss 1974: 84; for date cf. Johnson 1994: 147).

67 Epigraphic Survey 1998: xviii.
68 Brand 1999: 118–20.
69 Epigraphic Survey 1998: 65–75.
70 Porter and Moss 1972: 457–59.
71 Louvre C55: see n. 52, just above.
72 Porter and Moss 1960–64: 550–51; Schaden 1984; 2000.
73 Given that he was a senior officer early in Akhenaten's reign, he would probably have been at least fifty at Tutankhamun's accession, and sixty when he himself became king—quite possibly older, especially if he were a sibling of Queen Tiye.
74 Cf. Kákosy 1976.
75 The only other incorporation of an image of a queen into the decoration of a king's tomb is the slightly problematic labeling of a minor figure in KV14 (Porter and Moss 1960–64: 530[28, II]); images of women shown in Amenmeses' KV10 derive from a later reuse of the tomb (see Dodson 1987).
76 For a fragmentary fishing and fowling scene in the temple of Hatshepsut at Deir el-Bahari, see Porter and Moss 1972: 342[7]; hunting scenes are also found at Rameses III's Medinet Habu temple: ibid. 516[185], and were doubtless present in most other memorial temples as well.
77 One who may have also worked on the tombs of Horemheb and Rameses I: Robins 1994: 157–59.
78 Cf. Dodson and Ikram 2008: 252–55.
79 Cf. Eaton-Krauss 1993: 5–8.
80 Schaden 1984: 49–51 argues erroneously that the box of the sarcophagus was reversed: see Reeves 1990a: 71, pl. v.
81 Schaden 1984: 50–51.
82 Cf. Dodson 1994a: 119–28.
83 Schaden 1984: 54–57.
84 See p. 119, below.
85 With Schaden 1984: 59–62, against Reeves 1990a: 72, who would date the desecration to the early Nineteenth Dynasty; cf. Hari 1984.
86 See pp. 66, 108, above; cf. Reeves 1981; 1990a: 72–75. Schaden 1984: 59 would prefer to attribute this robbers' cache to a robbery of WV23 during the time between the interment and the desecration, while Reeves is non-commital (1990a: 75).
87 Human remains were found in both WV23 and the nearby WV25, but no evidence for their identity has yet been forthcoming (cf. Schaden 1984: 63).
88 In situ and BM EA117 (Porter and Moss 1939: 25[229–230]; 35–36[27]).
89 Cairo CG34516 (Porter and Moss 1974–81: 666).
90 See p. 129, below.
91 Turin S.5162 (Schiaparelli 1924: 55, 103, fig. 82[6]; Hari 1979).
92 Cf. Leblanc 1993.

Chapter 7: The Hawk in Festival

1 Davies 1903–08: V, 15, pl. xiii.
2 Martin 1989b: 9–15; when this was written the full extent of the forecourt of the tomb was not yet apparent: cf. Raven 2002 and forthcoming.
3 Porter and Moss 1972: 356[74, 2].

4 Turin C. 1379: Malek 1999: 58–59[800–642–650].

5 Porter and Moss 1974–81: 832

6 Porter and Moss 1972: 6.

7 Gardiner 1947: II, 106*–108*[387A].

8 Cf. the justification for Sethnakhte's seizure of power in the Great Harris Papyrus: "But the gods then inclined themselves to peace so as to put the land in its proper state in accordance with its normal condition, and they established their son, who came forth from their flesh" (pBM EA9999: Grandet 2005: I, 335; II, 226–33, pl. 76, l. 6–7); on his own Elephantine stela, Sethnakhte claims that he was "selected [by the god] from among the millions" (Kitchen 1968–90: V, 271–72, l. 5).

9 Dodson 1990: 88, cf. 91–96; as well as *iry-pʿt*, used for the crown prince at least from the early Nineteenth Dynasty, cf. pp. 101–102.

10 Darnell and Manassa 2007: 55 assume that the nominating pharaoh was Tutankhamun.

11 Analyzed by Gardiner, 1953b: 22–28.

12 Cf. Brand 1999: 120–23.

13 See p. 98, above.

14 The very old idea, still occasionally quoted, that their marriage is mentioned in the coronation inscription, has long been shown to be a reference to the goddess Werethekau, rather than the *ḥmt-nsw-wrt* (see Gardiner 1953b: 19).

15 Martin 1989b: 106[91], 114[112a]; Schneider 1996: 16[56], 75[St. 1, 2].

16 As is tacitly admitted by Martin, ibid.

17 Martin 1982: 275–76; Schneider 1996: 4, 27[129, 130].

18 In contrast, Strouhal and Callender 1992 argue that a Mutnodjmet mentioned on Cairo stela CG34187 was the future queen, with the stela thus implying her marriage to Horemheb in Year 3 of Ay.

19 Martin 1989b: 53, 108–109, pl. 49, 124, 151–53; Schneider 1996: 75[St. 1–3]; Raven et al. (forthcoming): chap. ix, which adds BM EA36 to the list of items from the tomb, as a fragment found at the tomb fits a missing part of that statue.

20 The remains of two female skeletons were found in the approach corridor to the burial chamber in question (Strouhal 2008: 4–5[N3–4]).

21 Schneider 1996: 18–19[61–66].

22 Martin 1989b: 147.

23 Schneider 1996: 12[25ab; 27a–b], correcting Martin 1982: 276.

24 Cf. p. 131, below, on how far wine vintages may relate to dates of burial.

25 Cf. Hari 1965; Strouhal and Callender 1992.

26 Porter and Moss 1972: 2.

27 Schneider 1996: 77–78[St. 10], pl. 86, 87, 103.

28 Porter and Moss 1937: 115 (called Mutemwia); Hari 1965: 207–208; Aldred 1968b: 103–106; 1970b; Schmidt 1994.

29 Porter and Moss 1972: 459.

30 Porter and Moss 1972: 187–88[582–83].

31 Epigraphic Survey 1994: 30–31, pl. 76, 82, 83.

32 Now destroyed: Porter and Moss 1960–64: 340[5].

33 The statue has also been ascribed to Rameses II's wife, Nefertiry D (cf. Schmidt 1974). However, the statue works stylistically far better for Mutnodjmet than for a later date.

34 Cf. Morkot 1986; Troy 1986: 65–66.

35 Porter and Moss 1952: 166.

36 Tiye is also a sphinx, trampling ememies, on the side of her throne as shown in TT192 (Epigraphic Survey 1980: 48–49).

37 Martin 1982.

38 Martin 1989b: 150–55, a complex often claimed to be of royal dimensions, but in fact comparable to the substructures of the tombs of other nobles of the late Eighteenth Dynasty and early Nineteenth Dynasty at Thebes (cf. Dodson and Ikram 2008: 225–28, 246, 265).

39 Strouhal 2008: 1–4[N1–2].

40 The formula on this piece is unusual, as is the addition to her titulary—uniquely for a queen—of Chantress of Amun (Schneider 1996: 44[261]).

41 Schneider 1996: 12[22–23].

42 Schneider 1996: 12[25a–b, 27a–b]; cf. p. 115, above.

43 BM EA36635.

44 Martin 1982: 277; Schneider 1996: 44; Thomas 1967 once suggested that she might be the owner of tomb QV33 in the Valley of the Queens; see, however Leblanc and Hassanein 1985: 27–28.

45 Cairo CG34162.

46 Porter and Moss 1972: 187[581]; Kruchten 1981.

47 Probably Tell el-Hebua, near El-Qantara.

48 Cf. Poláček 1976; Allam 2000.

49 Eaton-Krauss 1988: 11; *pace* Ratié 1986.

50 Johnson 1992: 136–37; it is unclear at what point the figures of Ay as a private person (p. 67, above) were erased, as it has been suggested that this could have been done following Ay's accession: cf. p. 155 n. 65.

51 Cross 2008, 2009: 19; he also argues (2009: 17–18) that the lack of cartouches within the seals used for resealing the tomb, contrasting with those used for the initial sealing and those used under Horemheb's to reseal KV43 (see just below), might imply that they were made during the "Zanzanzash Affair" interregnum.

52 Cf. Chapter 5, above.

53 Porter and Moss 1960–64: 560[4]; Reeves 1990a: 36–37.

54 Porter and Moss 1960–64: 567–69; Hornung 1971.

55 BM EA55624: Blackman 1926: 177, pl. xxxiv.

56 Cf. the extension of the village during the early Nineteenth Dynasty (Meskell 2000: 263).

57 Cf. p. 152 n. 9, above.

58 The well room, the antechamber, and the burial hall.

59 His KV17 (Porter and Moss 1960–64: 535–45; Hornung 1991) is the first royal tomb to be decorated from the very entrance, with all surfaces adorned; only one room (F) had not yet been carved and painted, its images being left in the black outline that preceded carving. In addition the lower walls of a stairway (B) were only partly carved (cf. Hornung 1991: pl. 78–95, 2–40).

60 Brand 2000: 305–309.

61 Porter and Moss 1972: 457–60.

62 See p. 152 n. 117, above.

63 Cf. Martin 1989b: 73 on the non-comprehensiveness of this activity, and the option that it might have been done after Horemheb's death.

64 E.g., Louvre N.412 (Porter and Moss 1974–81: 784).

65 Dodson 1997.

66 Martin 1989b: 88, 97, pl. 108, 115.

67 Porter and Moss 1974–81: 781–82; Dodson 1999: 62–63; 2005b: 73, 77.

68 See p. 74, above.

69 Cairo CG34175 (Porter and Moss 1934: 63).

70 Cairo (Porter and Moss 1934: 70).

71 See pp. 73–74, above.

72 Porter and Moss 1974–81: 832, 845, 850, 870; cf. p. 73, above, for his usurpation of a building of Tutankhamun at Memphis.

73 Borchardt 1910: II, 101, fig. 123; cf. pp. 73, 104, above, for items from the reigns of Tutankhamun and Ay.

74 BM EA58468 (Pendlebury 1951: pl. lx[3]; Bierbrier 1982: 9, pl. 2–3).

75 Petrie 1894: 43, pl. xi[5].

76 BM EA58468b-d, 58469 (Bierbrier 1982: 9, pl. 1; 1993: 7, pl. 1); the texts on EA58468d have been erased, perhaps in error in Ramesside times by those mutilating the other royal names present in the temple.

77 Pendlebury 1951: 12.

78 Spencer 1989: 15–22, 46–48.

79 Roeder 1969; Spencer 1989: 26–28, 46–48.

80 Peet and Wooley 1923: 125–34, 158–60.

81 Cairo Ex. 6018–6019 (inc. JE49536—Porter and Moss 1937: 90).

82 Porter and Moss 1937: 144; cf. Redford 1973c: 83 on Akhenaten blocks found at Medamud.

83 The latter begun by Amenhotep III.

84 Porter and Moss 1972: 39–41.

85 Brand 2000: 197–201, 211–12, who dates the whole hall to the reign of Sethy I.

86 Porter and Moss 1972: 186–91.

87 Porter and Moss 1972: 180–83.

88 Johnson 1992: 124–29, 169–86[49–72]. Darnell and Manassa suggest (2007: 182) that these reliefs actually refer to Horemheb's campaigning on behalf of Tutankhamun.

89 Van Siclen 2005a; 2005b; Carlotti 2005.

90 Cf. Le Saout 1982b.

91 Epigraphic Survey 1998: xvii.

92 Hayes 1951: 239, fig. 37[B].

93 Mond and Myers 1934: III, 51; III, pl. lv[56].

94 Porter and Moss 1937: 208–213; Klemm 1988: 41–45; Thiem 2000.

95 Porter and Moss 1937: 208.

96 Cf. Aldred 1971: 40; Darnell and Manassa 2007: 122–25.

97 Porter and Moss 1952: 119–21; Černý and Edel [1963]b. This temple, sadly, is now lost under Lake Nasser, save a few fragments preserved in the Nubian Museum, Aswan.

98 Porter and Moss 1952: 81.

99 Porter and Moss 1960–64: 95; Hari 1985: pl. vi, lv–lvii.

100 Cairo JE44863–4: Porter and Moss 1972: 188[584]; Delvaux 1992.

101 It has been suggested that this man is also named on stela Chicago OI 11456 (Cruz-Uribe 1978; for doubts see van Dijk in Martin 1997: 61 n. 4)

102 Thutmose was Overseer of the Priests of Upper Egypt and Lower Egypt (*imt-r ḥm-nṯr m šmˁw tȝ-mḥw*, Dodson 1990: 88).

103 Paramessu is presumably not to be identified with the Scribe of the Army Ramose, who appears as Horemheb's adjutant in his Saqqara tomb (Martin 1989b: 57, 84–85, pl. 53–54, 96–97). On the other hand, it has been suggested that Paramessu may have spelled his name "Ramose" at some point in his career—before becoming "Rameses" as king; cf. sources in next note.

104 Cairo JE60539 (the Year 400 Stela, Porter, and Moss 1934: 23); on this and Paramessu's broader family background, see Gaballa and Kitchen 1968, Goedicke 1981, van Dijk in Martin 1997: 60–62 and Brand 2000: 336–43.

105 Cairo JE36329: Porter and Moss 1972: 77.

106 Cf. van Dijk 1990: 25–26; 1993: 76–79.

107 Louvre N.1538 (Porter and Moss 1974–81: 663).

108 Turin C.6347 (Porter and Moss 1974–81: 773–74; Donadoni-Roveri (ed.) 1987: pl. 221–22).

109 Porter and Moss 1960–64: 339–40.

110 Wildung 1977: 1260; Maystre 1992: 281–84[79–81], 287–90[88–92].

111 Bierbrier 1977: 1243.

112 Cf. von Beckerath 1995, van Dijk 1995, and the various studies cited below.

113 A "Year 16" on a stone basin (Redford 1973a–b) is certainly part of a wholly-forged inscription.

114 van Dijk 2008.

115 See Schneider 1996 and van Dijk 2008: 12[22–23]

116 Porter and Moss 1974–81: 553–55.

117 Gaballa 1977: 25, pl. lvii, lxiii[S8].

118 There is absolutely no evidence that Horemheb did anything like this himself, although the idea is implicitly endorsed by Darnell and Manassa 2007: 56.

119 Depending on the number of odd months involved. It could potentially creep up to thirty-two if Ay lived significantly beyond his last recorded date.

120 Or perhaps twenty-eight, depending on how long Ay lived.

121 Cf. Gardiner 1938.

122 Harris 1968: 97.

123 Hölscher 1939: 106–108, fig. 89–90, pl. 51[c].

124 Which would require an independent reign for Neferneferuaten or an extension of the reigns of Tutankhamun and/or Ay to square with the Mose inscription.

125 Cf. Redford 1966: 122–23; Harris 1968: 96. Krauss 1994 suggests the date might be that of a feast marking Horemheb's accession day (cf. just below).

126 *Pace* Redford 1973a: 7.

127 *Pace* Harris 1968: 95; cf. Waddell 1940: 102–19.

128 van Dijk 2008.

129 Assuming that the Saqqara burial was indeed Mutnodjmet.

130 Černý 1965: 3–4, 24, pl. v[25]; cf. Tallet 1996.

131 One strongly suspects that this would have been done wherever possible with bulky, low-value items, to minimize effort on the day of the funeral. Indeed, there is evidence for such pre-positioning in the form of oCM CG25504, which records the introduction of funerary furniture into Merenptah's tomb (KV8) in his Year 7, three years before his death (Reeves 1990a: 97).

132 IFAO 1254: Janssen 1984; Krauss 1994. The palaeographic evidence for dating the piece appears to be equivocal (cf. Janssen 1984: 305–306).

133 Krauss 1994.

134 Given that the recipient came into office somewhere between Years 15 and 30; Mini[nwy] is also mentioned in a papyrus (pCairo JE65739) written some time after Year 15 (Gardiner 1935: 142). He is not, however, to be identified with the scribe Mini[nwy] who is recorded as active in Year 30 of, presumably, Rameses II (Davies 1999:125 n. 535).

135 Toronto A.11, II:12 (Gardiner 1913: 16g–k).

136 As does Harris 1968: 98–99.

137 Mininiwy's advanced age may be reflected by the phraseology he uses in the letter (cf. Gardiner 1913: 16g–k).

138 Harris 1968: 98.

139 Essentially TT50 (Neferhotep ii) and TT255 (Roy).

140 Cf. Harris 1968: 98.

141 Porter and Moss 1960–64: 15.

142 Porter and Moss 1960–64: 21.

143 Porter and Moss 1960–64: 50.

144 Porter and Moss 1972: 434[10.I.1].

145 Porter and Moss 1972: 500.

146 Cairo CG25646: cf. Philips 1977.

147 Hölscher 1939: 65.

148 Johnson 1992: 122–23.

149 On the basis of the paleography of a graffito on a statue base from the temple (Hölscher 1939: 107–108); cf. Johnson 1992: 123.

150 Martin 1989b: 70–72, pl. 68–71.

151 Cf. Martin 1989b: 72–73.

152 Yoyotte 1982–83: 148–49.

153 Leahy 1982: 72.

Chapter 8: Sunset

1 Edinburgh NMS A.1965.318 (Aldred 1968b: 100–102).

2 Gomaà 1973: 2–11.

3 Weeks 2000.

4 Epigraphic Survey 1979: pl. 26.

5 Cf. Dodson (forthcoming) b.

6 Johnson 1992: 83–135.

7 See pp. 86, 105, above.

8 Dodson and Ikram 2008: 247–69.

9 Brand 1999: 123–34.

10 Cf. Montserrat 2000.

APPENDICES

Appendix 1

Chronology of Ancient Egypt
LE = Lower Egypt only; UE = Upper Egypt.
All dates are more or less conjectural prior to 664 BC

Early Dynastic Period
Dynasty 1	3050–2810	BC
Dynasty 2	2810–2660	

Old Kingdom
Dynasty 3	2660–2600
Dynasty 4	2600–2470
Dynasty 5	2470–2360
Dynasty 6	2360–2195

First Intermediate Period
Dynasties 7/8	2195–2160
Dynasties 9/10 (LE)	2160–2040
Dynasty 11a (UE)	2160–2065

Middle Kingdom
Dynasty 11b	2065–1994
Dynasty 12	1994–1780
Dynasty 13	1780–1650

Second Intermediate Period

Dynasty 14 (LE)	1700–1650
Dynasty 15 (LE)	1650–1535
Dynasty 16 (UE)	1650–1590
Dynasty 17 (UE)	1585–1545

New Kingdom

Dynasty 18	
Ahmose I	1545–1520
Amenhotep I	1520–1499
Thutmose I	1499–1489
Thutmose II	1489–1479
Thutmose III	1479–1425
(Hatshepsut	1472–1457)
Amenhotep II	1425–1399
Thutmose IV	1399–1389
Amenhotep III	1389–1349
Amenhotep IV/Akhenaten	1349–1333
(Smenkhkare	1337–1336)
(Neferneferuaten	1336–1329)
Tutankhaten/amun	1333–1324
Ay	1324–1320
Horemheb	1320–1291
Dynasty 19	
Rameses I	1291–1289
Sethy I	1289–1279
Ramesses II	1279–1212
Merenptah	1212–1202
Sethy II	1202–1196
(Amenmeses UE)	1201–1197
Siptah	1196–1190
Tawosret	1190–1188
Dynasty 20	1190–1063
Sethnakhte	1190–1186
Rameses III	1186–1154

Third Intermediate Period

Dynasty 21	1063–937
Dynasty 22	939–716
Dynasty 23	856–720
Dynasty 24	734–721
Dynasty 25	754–656

Saite Period

Dynasty 26	664–525

Late Period

Dynasty 27	521–405
Dynasty 28	404–399
Dynasty 29	399–380
Dynasty 30	380–342
Dynasty 31	342–332

Hellenistic Period

Dynasty of Macedonia	332–310
Dynasty of Ptolemy	310–30
Roman Period	30 BC–AD 395

Appendix 2

Relative Chronology of Egyptian and Foreign Kings of the Late Eighteenth and Early Nineteenth Dynasties

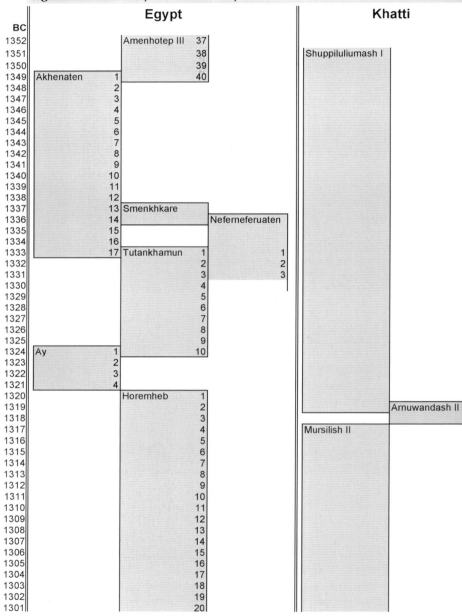

BC	Egypt			Khatti
1352		Amenhotep III	37	
1351			38	Shuppiluliumash I
1350			39	
1349	Akhenaten 1		40	
1348	2			
1347	3			
1346	4			
1345	5			
1344	6			
1343	7			
1342	8			
1341	9			
1340	10			
1339	11			
1338	12			
1337	13	Smenkhkare		
1336	14	Neferneferuaten		
1335	15			
1334	16			
1333	17	Tutankhamun 1	1	
1332		2	2	
1331		3	3	
1330		4		
1329		5		
1328		6		
1327		7		
1326		8		
1325		9		
1324	Ay 1	10		
1323	2			
1322	3			
1321	4			
1320		Horemheb 1		
1319		2		Arnuwandash II
1318		3		
1317		4		Mursilish II
1316		5		
1315		6		
1314		7		
1313		8		
1312		9		
1311		10		
1310		11		
1309		12		
1308		13		
1307		14		
1306		15		
1305		16		
1304		17		
1303		18		
1302		19		
1301		20		

Babylon	Assyria		BC
adashmanenlil I		Eriba-Adad	8	1352
Burnaburiash II			9	1351
	Assuruballit I	1	10	1350
		2		1349
		3		1348
		4		1347
		5		1346
		6		1345
		7		1344
		8		1343
		9		1342
		10		1341
		11		1340
		12		1339
		13		1338
		14		1337
		15		1336
		16		1335
		17		1334
		18		1333
		19		1332
		20		1331
		21		1330
		22		1329
		23		1328
		24		1327
		25		1326
rakhardash II		26		1325
		27		1324
	Nazibugash	28		1323
rigzalu II		29		1322
		30		1321
		31		1320
		32		1319
		33		1318
		34		1317
		35		1316
		36	Enlilnirari	1	1315
			2	1314
			3	1313
			4	1312
			5	1311
			6	1310
			7	1309
			8	1308
			9	1307
	Arikdenilu	1	10	1306
		2		1305
		3		1304
		4		1303
		5		1302
Nazimaruttash		6		1301

BC	Egypt				Khatti	
1300		Horemheb	21		Mursilish II	
1299			22			Muwatallish II
1298			23			
1297			24			
1296			25			
1295			26			
1294			27			
1293			28			
1292			29			
1291			30			
1290	Rameses I					
1289		Sethy I	1			
1288			2			
1287			3			
1286			4			
1285			5			
1284			6			
1283			7			
1282			8			
1281			9			
1280			10			
1279	Rameses II	1	11			
1278		2				
1277		3				
1276		4				
1275		5				
1274		6				
1273		7				
1272		8			Mushilish III	
1271		9			(Urhi-Teshub)	
1270		10				
1269		11				
1268		12				
1267		13				
1266		14				
1265		15				Hattushilish III
1264		16				
1263		17				

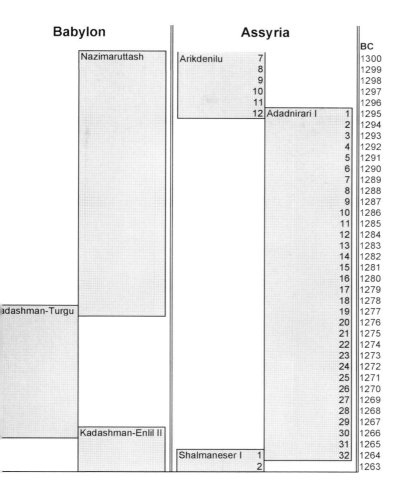

Babylon	Assyria		BC
Nazimaruttash	Arikdenilu	7	1300
		8	1299
		9	1298
		10	1297
		11	1296
		12 Adadnirari I 1	1295
		2	1294
		3	1293
		4	1292
		5	1291
		6	1290
		7	1289
		8	1288
		9	1287
		10	1286
		11	1285
		12	1284
		13	1283
		14	1282
		15	1281
		16	1280
		17	1279
		18	1278
adashman-Turgu		19	1277
		20	1276
		21	1275
		22	1274
		23	1273
		24	1272
		25	1271
		26	1270
		27	1269
		28	1268
		29	1267
		30	1266
		31	1265
Kadashman-Enlil II	Shalmaneser I 1	32	1264
		2	1263

Fig. 101. The culmination of the Egypto-Hittite relations: the marriage in Rameses II's year 34 between the king and a daughter of Hattushilish III, renamed on her arrival as Maathorneferure. This scene appears at the top of a stela commemorating the event outside the Great Temple at Abu Simbel.

Appendix 3

Royal Names of the Late Eighteenth Dynasty

Key: H. = Horus name;
      Nb. = Nebti name;
      G. = Golden Falcon name;
      P. = Prenomen;
      N. = Nomen

Amenhotep IV

H.	*k3-nḫt q3i-šwti*
Nb.	*wsr-nsyt-m-'Ipt-swt*
G.	*wts-ḥ'w-m-'Iwnw-šm'y*
P.	*nfr-ḫprw-R' w'-n-R'*
N.	*'Imn-ḥtp nṯr-ḥq3-W3st*

Akhenaten

H.	*mry-itn*
Nb.	*wsr-nsyt-m-3ḫt-'Itn*
G.	*wts-rn-n-'Itn*
P.	*nfr-ḫprw-R' w'-n-R'*
N.	*3ḫ-n-'Itn*

Smenkhkare

P.	*'nḫ-ḫprw-R'*
N.	*smnḫ-k3-R' ḏsr-ḫprw*

Nefernefruaten

Pa.	*'nḫ-ḫprw-R' mry-Nfrḫprwr'*
Na.	*nfr-nfrw-'Itn mry-W'nr'*
Pb.	*'nḫ-ḫprw-R' mry-W'nr'*
Nb.	*nfr-nfrw-'Itn 3ḫt-n-hi.s*
Pc.	*'nḫ-ḫprw-R' mry-Nfrḫprwr'*
Nc.	*nfr-nfrw-'Itn 3ḫt-n-hi.s*
Pd.	*'nḫ-ḫprw-R' mry-'I[...]*
Nd.	*nfr-nfrw-'Itn mry-'I[mn?]*
Pe.	*'nḫ-ḫprw-R' mry-'Itn*
Ne.	*nfr-nfrw-'Itn ḥq3*

Tutankhaten/amun

H.   *k3-nḫt twt-mswt*

Nb*a.*   *nfr-ḥpw sgrḥ-t3wy sḥtp-nṯrw-nbw*

Nb*b.*   *wr-ʿḥ ʾImn*

G.   *wṯs-ḫʿw sḥtp-nṯrw/it.f-Rʿ*

P.   *nb-ḫprw-Rʿ*

N*1.*   *twt-ʿnḫ-ʾItn*

N*2.*   *twt-ʿnḫ-ʾImn ḥq3-ʾIwnw-šmʿy*

Ay

H.   *k3-nḫt ṯhn-ḫʿw/ḫprw*

Nb.   *sḥm-pḥty dr-Sṯtiw*

G.   *ḥq3-M3ʿt sḫpr-t3wy*

P.   *ḫpr-ḫprw-Rʿ iri-M3ʿt*

N.   *it-nṯr iy nṯr-ḥq3-W3st*

Horemheb

H.   *k3-nḫt spd-sḫrw*

Nb.   *wr-bi3wt-m-ʾIptswt*

G.   *ḥrw-ḥr-M3ʿt sḫpr-t3wy*

P.   *dsr-ḫprw-Rʿ stp-n-Rʿ*

N.   *Ḥr-m-ḥb mr-n-ʾImn*

Nefertiti

1.   *nfrt-iy-ti*

2.   *nfr-nfrw-itn nfrt-iy-ti*

Appendix 4

Tentative Genealogy of the Late Eighteenth Dynasty

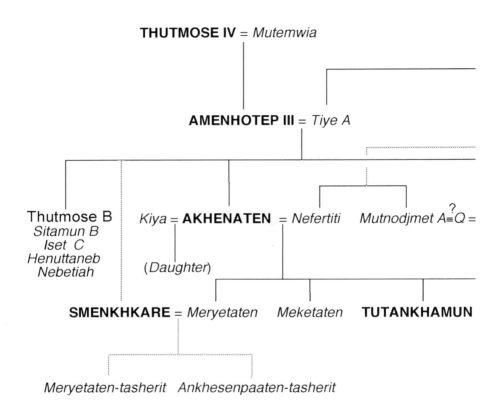

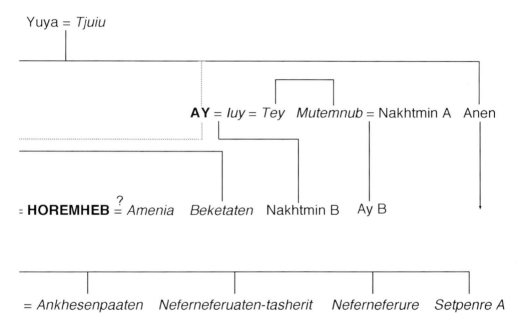

Yuya = *Tjuiu*

AY = *Iuy* = *Tey*   *Mutemnub* = Nakhtmin A   Anen

≡ **HOREMHEB** =[?] *Amenia*   *Beketaten*   Nakhtmin B   Ay B

= *Ankhesenpaaten*   *Neferneferuaten-tasherit*   *Neferneferure*   *Setpenre A*

BIBLIOGRAPHY

Abbreviations for Periodicals

AL	*Amarna Letters* (San Francisco; Sebastopol: KMT Communications).
AncEg	*Ancient Egypt* (Manchester: Ancient Egypt Magazine).
AO	*Acta Orientalia* (Copenhagen: Munksgaard).
ASAE	*Annales du Service des Antiquités de l'Égypte* (Cairo: Institut français d'Archéologie orientale; Supreme Council of Antiquities Press).
BACE	*Bulletin of the Australian Centre for Egyptology* (North Ryde: Australian Centre for Egyptology, Macquarie University).
BASOR	*Bulletin of the American Schools of Oriental Research* (Ann Arbor: American Schools of Oriental Research).
BES	*Bulletin of the Egyptological Seminar* (New York: Egyptological Seminar of New York).
BIFAO	*Bulletin de l'Institut français d'Archéologie orientale du Caire* (Cairo: Institut français d'Archéologie orientale).
BSEG	*Bulletin de la Société d'Égyptologie de Genève* (Geneva: Societé d'Égyptologie de Genève).
BSFE	*Bulletin de la Societé français d'Egyptologie* (Paris: Societé français d'Egyptologie).
Cairo	Egyptian Museum, Cairo.
CdE	*Chronique d'Egypte* (Brussels: Fondation égyptologique Reine Elisabeth).

DE	*Discussions in Egyptology* (Oxford: DE Publications).
EgArch	*Egyptian Archaeology: Bulletin of the Egypt Exploration Society* (London: Egypt Exploration Society).
GM	*Göttinger Miszellen* (Göttingen: Universität Göttingen. Ägyptologisches Seminar).
JARCE	*Journal of the American Research Center in Egypt* (New York, &c: Eisenbraun).
JCS	*Journal of Cuneiform Studies* (Cambridge, MA: American Schools of Oriental Research).
JEA	*Journal of Egyptian Archaeology* (London: Egypt Exploration Fund/Society).
JNES	*Journal of Near Eastern Studies* (Chicago: Chicago University Press).
JSSEA	*Journal of the Society for the Study of Egyptian Antiquities* (Toronto: Society for the Study of Egyptian Antiquities).
Kmt	*Kmt: A Modern Journal of Ancient Egypt* (San Francisco, &c: Kmt Communications).
KUB	*Keilschrifturkunden aus Boghazköi*, 60 vols (Berlin: Akademie Verlag, 1921–1990).
LÄ	*Lexikon der Ägyptologie* (Wiesbaden: Otto Harrassowitz, 1975ff.).
LAAA	*Annals of Archaeology and Anthropology* (Liverpool: Institute of Archaeology).
MDAIK	*Mitteilungen des Deutschen Archäologischen Instituts, Kairo* (Mainz: Philipp von Zabern).
MDOG	*Mitteilungen der Deutschen Orient-Gesellschaft* (Berlin: Deutschen Orient-Gesellschaft).
NSSEA	*Newsletter of the Society for the Study of Egyptian Antiquities* (Toronto: Society for the Study of Egyptian Antiquities).
OLZ	*Orientalistische Literaturzeitung* (Leipzig: Hinrichs; Berlin: Akademie Verlag).
OMRO	*Oudheidkundige Mededelingen uit het Rijksmuseum van Oudheden te Leiden* (Leiden: Rijksmuseum van Oudheden).
RdE	*Revue d'Egyptologie* (Leuven: Peeters).
SAK	*Studien zur altägyptschen Kultur* (Hamburg: H. Buske Verlag).
VA	*Varia Aegyptica* (San Antonio, TX: Van Siclen Books).
ZÄS	*Zeitschrift für Ägyptische Sprache und Altertumskunde* (Leipzig: J.C. Hinrichs'sche Buchhandlung; Berlin: Akademie Verlag).

Aldred, C. 1957. "The End of the El-'Amārna Period." *JEA* 43: 30–41.

——— 1959. "The Beginning of the El-'Amarna Period." *JEA* 45: 19–33.

——— 1968a. *Akhenaten, Pharaoh of Egypt*. London: Thames & Hudson.

——— 1968b. "Two Monuments of the Reign of Ḥoremḥeb." *JEA* 54: 100–106.

——— 1969. "The 'New Year' Gifts to the Pharaoh." *JEA* 55: 73–81.

——— 1970a. "The Foreign Gifts Offered to Pharaoh." *JEA* 56: 105–16.

——— 1970b. "Queen Mutnodjme—a Correction." *JEA* 56: 195–96.

——— 1971. "Egypt: The Amarna Period and the End of the Eighteenth Dynasty." In *Cambridge Ancient History*, 2nd ed., vol. 2, ch. xix. Cambridge: Cambridge University Press.

——— 1988. *Akhenaten, King of Egypt*. London: Thames & Hudson.

Allam, S. 2000. "Der Steuer-Erlass des Königs Haremheb (Urk. IV 2156, 17 ff.)." *ZÄS* 127: 103–11.

Allen, J.P. 1988. "Two Altered Inscriptions of the Late Amarna Period." *JARCE* 25: 117–21.

——— 1991. "Akhenaten's 'Mystery' Coregent and Successor." *Amarna Letters* 1: 74–85.

——— 1994. "Nefertiti and Smenkh-ka-re." *GM* 141: 7–17.

——— 2006. "The Amarna Succession." In *Causing His Name to Live: Studies in Egyptian Epigraphy and History in Memory of William J. Murnane*, edited by P. Brand. <http://history.memphis.edu/murnane/>.

Amer, A.A.M.A. 1985. "Tutankhamun's Decree for the Chief Treasurer Maya." *RdE* 36: 17–20.

Arnold, Do. 1996. "Aspects of the Royal Female Image during the Amarna Period." In *The Royal Women of Amarna: Images of Beauty from Ancient Egypt*, edited by Do. Arnold, 85–119. New York: Metropolitan Museum of Art.

Aston, D.A. and J.D. Bourriau (in preparation) *The Memphite Tomb of Horemheb, Commander-in-Chief of Tutankhamun*, III: *The Pottery*. London: Egypt Exploration Society.

Aston, D.A. and B.G. Aston. (in preparation) *The Tomb of Maya and Meryt*, III: *The Pottery*.

Azim, M. 1982. "La structure des pylônes d'Horemheb à Karnak." *Cahiers de Karnak*, vol. 7, 127–66. Paris: Éditions Recherche sur les Civilisations.

Bell, L. 1985. "Aspects of the Cult of the Deified Tutankhamun." In *Mélanges Gamal Eddin Mokhtar*, edited by P. Posener-Krièger, vol. 1, 31–59. Cairo: Institut français d'Archéologie orientale.

Bell, M.R. 1990. "An Armchair Excavation of KV 55." *JARCE* 27: 97–137.

———— 1938. "A Later Allusion to Akhenaten." *JEA* 24: 124.

———— 1947. *Ancient Egyptian Onomastica*. 3 vols. Oxford: Oxford University Press.

———— 1952. "Tuthmosis III Returns Thanks to Amun." *JEA* 38: 6–23.

———— 1953a. "The Tomb of the General Ḥaremḥab." *JEA* 39: 3–12.

———— 1953b. "The Coronation of King Ḥaremḥab." *JEA* 39: 13–31.

Germer, R. 2001. "Die Mumie aus dem Sarg in »KV55«." In *Das Geheimnis des goldenen Sarges: Echnaton und das Ende der Amarnazeit*, edited by G. Grimm and S. Schoske, 58–61. Munich: Lipp Verlag.

Giles, F.J. 1970. *Ikhnaton: Legend and History*. London: Hutchinson.

———— 2001. *The Amarna Age: Egypt*. Warminster: Aris & Phillips.

Glanville, S.R.K. 1927. "Note on the Nature and Date of the 'Papyri' of Nakht, B. M. 10471 and 10473." *JEA* 13: 50–56.

Goedicke, H. 1981. "The '400-Year Stela' Reconsidered." *BES* 3: 25–42.

Gohary, J. 1992. *Akhenaten's Sed-festival at Karnak*. London and New York: Kegan Paul International.

Goldwasser, O. 1990. "A Cartouche of Semenekhkare from Canaan." *GM* 115: 29–32.

Gomaà, F. 1973. *Chaemwese, Sohn Ramses' II und Hoherpriester von Memphis*. Weisbaden: Otto Harrassowitz.

Grajetzki, W. 2006. *The Middle Kingdom of Ancient Egypt*. London: Duckworth.

Grandet, P. 2005. *Le Papyrus Harris I (BM 9999)*. 2 vols. 2nd ed., Cairo: Institut français d'Archéologie orientale.

Grimm, A. 2001. "Goldsarg ohne Geheimnis: Interpretation des Aitopsiebefundes." In *Das Geheimnis des goldenen Sarges: Echnaton und das Ende der Amarnazeit*, edited by G. Grimm and S. Schoske, 101–20. Munich: Lipp Verlag.

Grimm, A. and S. Schoske (eds.). 2001. *Das Geheimnis des goldenen Sarges: Echnaton und das Ende der Amarnazeit*. Munich: Lipp Verlag.

Güterbock, H.G. 1956. "The Deeds of Suppiluliuma as Told by His Son, Mursili II." *JCS* X: 41–68, 75–98, 107–30.

Habachi, L. 1958. "God's Fathers and the Role They Played in the History of the First Intermediate Period." *ASAE* 55: 167–90.

————1979. "Unknown or Little-known Monuments of Tutankhamun and His Viziers." In *Glimpses of Ancient Egypt: Studies in Honour of H.W. Fairman*, edited by J. Ruffle, G.A. Gaballa and K.A. Kitchen, 32–41. Warminster: Aris & Phillips.

———— 1980. "Königssohn von Kusch." *LÄ* III: 630–40.

Habachi, L. and P. Anus. 1977. *Le tombeau de Naÿ à Gournet Mar'eï (No. 271)*. Cairo: Institut français d'Archéologie orientale.

Hanke, R. 1978. *Amarna-Reliefs aus Hermopolis. Neue Veröffentlichungen und Studien.* Hildesheim: Gerstenberg Verlag.

Hari, R. 1965. *Horemheb et la reine Moutnedjemet ou la fin d'une dynastie.* Geneva: Editions de Belles-Lettres.

———— 1976. "La reine d'Horemheb était-elle la soeur de Nefertiti?" *CdE* LI/101: 39–46.

———— 1979. "Mout-Nefertari, épouse de Ramses II: une descendante de l'hérétique Ai?" *Aegyptus* 59: 3–7.

———— 1984. "La 'damnatio memoriae' amarnienne." In *Mélanges Adolphe Gutbub*, 95–102. Montpellier: Université de Montpellier.

———— 1985. *La tombe thébaine du père divin Neferhotep (TT 50).* Geneva: Editions de Belles-Lettres.

Harris, J.R. 1968. "How long was the reign of Horemheb?" *JEA* 54: 95–99.

———— 1973a. "Neferneferuaten." *GM* 4: 15–17.

———— 1973b. "Neferneferuaten Rediviva." *AO* 35: 5–13.

———— 1973c. "The date of the 'Restoration' stela of Tutankhamun." *GM* 5: 9–11.

———— 1974. "Neferneferuaten Regnans." *AO* 36: 11–21.

———— 1977. "Akhenaten or Nefertiti?" *AO* 38: 5–10.

———— 1992. "Akhenaten and Neferneferuaten." In *After Tut'ankhamūn*, edited by C.N. Reeves, 55–72. London and New York: Kegan Paul International.

Harrison, R.G. 1966. "An Anatomical Examination of the Pharaonic Remains Purported to be Akhenaten." *JEA* 52: 95–119.

Harrison, R.G., R.C. Connolly, and A. Abdalla. 1969. "Kinship of Smenkhkare and Tutankhamen Demonstrated Serologically." *Nature* 224: 325–26.

Harrison, R.G., R.C. Connolly, S. Ahmed, A.B. Abdalla, and M. el Ghawaby. 1979. "A Mummified Foetus from the Tomb of Tutankhamun." *Antiquity* 53: 19–21.

Hasegawa, S. 2003. "The New Kingdom Necropolis at Dahshur." In *Egyptology at the Dawn of the Twenty-First Century: Proceedings of the Eighth International Congress of Egyptologists, Cairo, 2000*, edited by Z. Hawass and L.P. Brock, vol. 1, 229–33. Cairo: The American University in Cairo Press.

Hawass, Z. 2005. *Tutankhamun and the Golden Age of the Pharaohs.* Washington, DC: National Geographic Society.

———— 2009. "Dig days: King Tut was the son of Akhenaten." *Al-Ahram Weekly* 929.

Hayes, W.C. 1951. "Inscriptions from the Palace of Amenhotep III." *JNES* 10: 35–111, 156–83, 231–42.

Helck, W. 1955–58. *Urkunden der 18. Dynastie*, 17–22. Berlin: Akademie-Verlag.

———— 1973. "Probleme der Zeit Haremhebs." *CdE* XLVIII/96: 251–65.

———— 1984. "Kijê." *MDAIK* 40: 159–67.

———— 2001. *Das Grab Nr. 55 im Königsgräbertal. Sein Inhalt und seine historische Bedeutung*. Mainz: Philipp von Zabern.

Hoffmeier, J.K. 2006. "Recent Excavations on the 'Ways of Horus.'" *ASAE* 80: 257–79.

Hoffmeier, J.K. and M. Abd el-Maksoud. 2003. "A New Military Site on the 'Ways of Horus' — Tell el-Borg 1999–2001: A Preliminary Report." *JEA* 89: 169–97.

Hölscher, U. 1939. *The Excavation of Medinet Habu*, II: *The Temples of the Eighteenth Dynasty*. Chicago: University of Chicago Press.

Hornung, E. 1971. *Das Grab des Haremhab im Tal der Könige*. Bern: Francke Verlag.

———— 1991. *The Tomb of Pharaoh Seti I. Das Grab Sethos' I*. Zürich and Munich: Artemis Verlag.

———— 1999. *Akhenaten and the religion of light*. Ithaca, NY: Cornell University Press.

Ikram, S. 1989. "Domestic Shrines and the Cult of the Royal Family at el-'Amarna." *JEA* 75: 89–101.

James, T.G.H. 1974. *Corpus of Hieroglyphic Inscriptions in The Brooklyn Museum*, I. *From Dynasty I to the End of Dynasty XVIII*. Brooklyn: The Brooklyn Museum.

Janssen. J.J. 1984. "A curious error (O. Institut français d'Archéologie orientale. 1254)." *BIFAO* 84: 303–306.

Johnson, W.R. 1992. *An Asiatic Battle Scene of Tutankhamun from Thebes: a late Amarna antecedent of the Ramesside battle narrative tradition*. PhD thesis, University of Chicago. Ann Arbor: UMI.

———— 1994. "Hidden Kings and Queens of the Luxor Temple Cachette." *Amarna Letters* 3: 128–49.

———— 1996. "Amenhotep III and Amarna: Some New Considerations." *JEA* 82: 65–82.

———— 1998. "Monuments and Monumental Art under Amenhotep III." In *Amenhotep III: perspectives on his reign*, edited by D.B. O'Connor and E.H. Cline, 63–94. Ann Arbor: University of Michigan Press.

———— 2009–2010. "The Battle Reliefs of Tutankhamen," *Kmt* 20/4.

Jones, D. 2000. *An Index of Ancient Egyptian Titles, Epithets and Phrases of the Old Kingdom*. Oxford: Archaeopress.

Kaiser, W. 1967. *Ägyptisches Museum Berlin*. Berlin: Staatliche Museen Berlin.

Kákosy, L. 1976. "Some Remarks on Tutankhamun's Tomb." In *Тутанхамон и его Время*, 31–34. Moscow: Nauka.

Kampp, F. 1996. *Die thebanische Nekropole: zum Wandel des Grabgedankens von der XVIII. bis zur XX. Dynastie.* 2 vols. Mainz: Phillipp von Zabern.

Kemp, B.J. 1987. "The Amarna Workmen's Village in Retrospect." *JEA* 73: 21–50.

———— 1989. *Ancient Egypt: Anatomy of a Civilization.* 1st ed., London: Routledge.

———— 2004. "Tell el-Amarna, 2004." *JEA* 60: 14–26.

———— 2006. *Ancient Egypt: Anatomy of a Civilization.* 2nd ed., London: Routledge.

———— 2008/9. "The Amarna Project: Why Amarna Died." *AncEg* 9/3: 44–51.

El-Khouli, A.A.H., R. Holthoer, C.A. Hope and O.E. Kaper. 1993. *Stone Vessels, Pottery and Sealings from the Tomb of Tut'ankhamūn.* Oxford: Griffith Institute.

El-Khouly, A. and G.T. Martin. 1987. *Excavations in the Royal Necropolis at El-'Amarna 1984.* Cairo: Egyptian Antiquities Organization.

Kitchen, K.A. 1962. *Suppiluliuma and the Amarna Pharaohs. A Study in Relative Chronology.* Liverpool: Liverpool University Press.

———— 1968–90. *Ramesside Inscriptions: Historical and Biographical.* Oxford: Blackwell.

———— 1985. Review of Krauss 1978, *JEA* 71 *Reviews Supplement*: 43–44.

———— 1995. *The Third Intermediate Period in Egypt (1100–650 B.C.),* 3rd ed. Warminster: Aris & Phillips.

Klemm, R. 1988. "Vom Steinbruch zum Tempel. Beobachtungen zur Baustruktur einiger Felstempel der 18. und 19. Dynastie im ägyptischen Mutterland." *ZÄS* 115: 41–51.

Kozloff, A.P. 2006. "Bubonic Plague During the Reign of Amenhotep III?" *Kmt* 17/3: 36–46, 83.

Krauss, R. 1978. *Das Ende der Amarnazeit.* Hildesheim: Gerstenberg.

———— 1986. "Kija–ursprüngliche Besitzerin der Kanopen aus KV 55." *MDAIK* 42: 67–80.

———— 1989. "Neues zu den Stelenfragmenten UC London 410 + Kairo JE 64959." *BSEG* 13: 83–87.

———— 1994. "Nur ein kurioser Irrtum oder ein Beleg für die Jahre 26 und 27 von Haremhab." *DE* 30: 73–85.

———— 1997. "Zur Chronologie der Nachfolger Achenatens unter Berücksichtigung der DOG-Funde aus Amarna." *MDOG* 129: 242–44.

Krauss, R. and D. Ullrich. 1982. "Ein gläserner Doppelring aus Altägypten." *Jahrbuch Preussischer Kulturbesitz* 19: 199–212.

Kruchten, J.-M. 1981. *Le Décret d'Horemheb: traduction, commentaire épigraphique, philologique et institutionnel.* Brussels: Éditions de l'Université de Bruxelles.

Kuhlmann, K.P. 1979. "Der Felstempel des Eje bei Akhmim." *MDAIK* 35: 165–88.

Laroche, E. 1971. *Catalogue des textes hittites.* Paris: Klincksieck.

Larson, J.A. 1992. "The Tutankhamun Astronomical Instrument." *Amarna Letters* 2: 76–86.

Le Saout, F. 1982a. "Reconstitution des murs de la Cour de la Cachette." *Cahiers de Karnak VII: 1978–1981,* 213–58. Paris: Editions Recherche sur les civilisations.

———— 1982b, "Nouveaux fragments au nom d'Horemheb." *Karnak* VII: 259–63.

Leahy, A. 1982. "*Ḥnsw-iy*: A Problem of Late Onomastica." *GM* 60: 67–79.

———— 1984. "Saite Royal Sculptue: A Review." *GM* 80: 69–70.

Leblanc, C. 1993. "Isis-Nofret, grande épouse de Ramsès II. La reine, sa famille et Nofretari." *BIFAO* 93: 313–33.

Leblanc, C. and F. Hassanein. 1985. "La Vallée des Reines." *Archéologia* 205: 24–31.

Leek, F.F. 1972. *The Human Remains from the Tomb of Tutʿankhamūn.* Oxford: Griffith Institute.

Leprohon R.J. 1985. "The Reign of Akhenaten Seen through the Later Royal Decrees." In *Mélanges Gamal Eddin Mokhtar,* edited by P. Posener-Krièger, vol. 2, 93–103. Cairo: Institut français d'Archéologie orientale.

Lepsius, C.R. 1849–59. *Denkmaeler aus Aegypten und Aethiopien.* 6 vols. Berlin/Leipzig: Nicolaische Buchandlung.

———— 1897. *Denkmaeler aus Aegypten und Aethiopien, Text,* edited by E. Naville, L. Borchardt and K. Sethe. Leipzig: J.C. Hinrichs.

Loeben, C.E. 1986. "Eine Bestattung der *großen königlichen Gemahlin Nofretete* in Amarna." *MDAIK* 42: 99–107.

———— 1991. "No Evidence of Coregency: Zwei getigte Inschriften aus dem Grab von Tutanchamun." *BSEG* 15: 82–90.

———— 1994. "No Evidence of Coregency: Two Erased Inscriptions from Tutankhamun's Tomb." *Amarna Letters* 3: 105–109.

———— 1999. "Une inhumation de la grande épouse royal Néfertiti à Amarna? La figurine funéraire de Néfertiti." *Égypte, Afrique et Orient* 13: 25–30.

Macadam, M.L. 1955. *The Temples of Kawa.* vol. 2. Oxford: Griffith Institute.

Málek, J. 1996. "The 'coregency relief' of Akhenaten and Smenkhkare from Memphis." In *Studies in Honor of William Kelly Simpson*, edited by P. Der Manuelian, vol. 2, 553–59. Boston: Museum of Fine Arts.

———— 1999. *Topographical Bibliography of Ancient Egyptian Hieroglyphic Texts, Reliefs and Paintings*, VIII/1–2: *Objects of Provenance Unknown, Statues*. Oxford: Griffith Institute.

Malinine, M., G. Posener and J. Vercoutter. 1968. *Catalogue des stèles du Sérapéum de Memphis*, I. Paris: Imprimerie Nationale.

Manniche, L. 1975. "The wife of Bata." *GM* 18: 33–38.

Martin, G.T. 1974, 1989a. *The Royal Tomb at El-'Amarna. The Rock Tombs of El-'Amarna, Part VII*, I, II. London: Egypt Exploration Society.

———— 1982. "Queen Mutnodjmet at Memphis and El-'Amarna." In *L'Égyptologie en 1979: Axes prioritaires de recherches*, vol. 2, 275–78. Paris.

———— 1986. "Shabtis of private persons in the Amarna Period." *MDAIK* 42: 109–29.

———— 1989b. *The Memphite Tomb of Horemheb, Commander-in-Chief of Tut'ankhamūn*, I. London: Egypt Exploration Society.

———— 1991a. *The Hidden Tombs of Memphis: new discoveries from the time of Tutankhamun and Ramesses the Great*. London: Thames & Hudson.

———— 1991b. *A Bibliography of the Amarna Period and its Aftermath. The Reigns of Akhnaten, Smenkhkare, Tutankhamun and Ay (c. 1350–1321 BC)*. London and New York: Kegan Paul International.

———— 1997. *The Tomb of Tia and Tia, a Royal Monument of the Ramesside Period in the Memphite Necropolis*. London: Egypt Exploration Society.

———— 2005. *Stelae from Egypt and Nubia in the Fitzwilliam Museum, Cambridge, c. 3000 BC–AD 1150*. Cambridge: Cambridge University Press.

Maystre, C. 1977. "Le grand-prêtre memphite du relief Berlin 12411." In *Ägypten und Kusch [Fritz Hintze zum 60. Geburtstag]*, edited by E. Endesfelde, 303–307. Berlin: Akademie-Verlag.

———— 1992. *Les grands prêtres de Ptah de Memphis*. Freiburg: Universitätsverlag/ Göttingen: Vandenhoeck & Ruprecht.

McLeod, W. 1970. *Composite Bows from the Tomb of Tut'ankhamūn*. Oxford: Griffith Institute.

Merrillees, R.S. 1987. *Alashia Revisited*. Paris: Gabalda.

Meskell, L. 2000. "Spatial Analyses of the Deir el-Medina Settlement and Necropoleis." In *Deir el-Medina in the Third Millennium AD: a tribute to Jac. J. Janssen*, edited by R.J. Demerée and A. Egberts, 259–75. Leiden: Nederlands Instituut voor het Nabije Oosten.

Mond, R. and O.H. Myers. 1934. *The Bucheum*. 3 vols. London: Egypt Exploration Society.

Molleson T. and M. Cox. 1993. *The Spitalfields Project*: II—*The Anthropology, The Middling Sort*. York: Council for British Archaeology.

Moran, W.L. 1992. *The Amarna Letters*. Baltimore and London: Johns Hopkins University Press.

Morkot, R. 1985. "Nakhtmin, the Supposed Viceroy of Ay." *Wepwawet* 1: 7–8.

———— 1986. "Violent Images of Queenship and the Royal Cult." *Wepwawet* 2: 1–9.

Montserrat, D. 2000. *Akhenaten: history, fantasy and ancient Egypt*. London and New York: Routledge.

Moseley, S. 2009. *Amarna: The Missing Evidence*. Calshot: Peach Pixel.

Moursi, M.I. 1972. *Die Hohenpriester des Sonnengottes von der Frühzeit Ägyptens bis zum Ende des Neuen Reiches*. Munich and Berlin: Deutscher Kunstverlag.

———— 1987. "Corpus der Mnevis-Stelen und Untersuchungen zum Kult der Mnevis-Stiere in Heliopolis. II." *SAK* 14: 225–37.

Munro, P. 1969. "Die Namen Semenech-ka-Re's. Ein Beitrag zur Liquidierung der Amarna-Zeit." *ZÄS* 95: 109–16.

Murnane, W.J. 1977a. *Ancient Egyptian Coregencies*. Chicago: Oriental Institute.

———— 1977b. Review of Martin 1974, *JNES* 36: 306–308.

———— 1979. "The Bark of Amun on the Third Pylon at Karnak." *JARCE* 16: 11–27.

———— 1985. "Tutankhamun on the Eighth Pylon at Karnak." *VA* 1: 59–68.

———— 1990. *The Road to Kadesh: A historical interpretation of the battle reliefs of King Sety I at Karnak*. 2nd ed. Chicago: Oriental Institute.

———— 1995. *Texts from the Amarna Period in Egypt*. Atlanta: Scholars Press.

———— 2001. "The End of the Amarna Period Once Again." *OLZ* 96: 9–22.

Murnane, W.J. and C.C. van Siclen III. 1993. *The Boundary Stelae of Akhenaten*. London and New York: Kegan Paul International.

Newberry, P.E. 1928. "Akhenaten's Eldest Son-in-Law 'Ankhkheperurē'." *JEA* 14: 3–9.

Nicholson, C. 1891. *Aegyptiaca*. London: Harrison.

Nims, C.F. 1973. "The Transition from the Traditional to the New Style of Wall Relief under Amenhotep IV." *JNES* 32: 181–87.

O'Connor, D.B. and E.H. Cline (eds). 1998. *Amenhotep III: Perspectives on his Reign*. Ann Arbor: University of Michigan Press.

Ockinga, B.G. 1994. "Another Ramesside Attestation of Usermont, Vizier of Tutankhamun." *BACE* 5: 61–66.

———— 1997. *A Tomb from the Reign of Tutankhamun at Akhmim*. Warminster: Aris & Phillips.

Pamminger, P. 1993. "Zur Göttlichkeit Amenophis' III." *BSEG* 17: 83–92.

Panagiotakopulu, E. 2004. "Pharaonic Egypt and the origins of plague." *Journal of Biogeography* 31: 269–75.

Pasquali, S. 2007. "La date du papyrus BM 10056." *RdE* 58: 71–85.

Peet, T.E. and C.L. Wooley. 1923. *City of Akhenaten*, I: *Excavations of 1921 and 1923 at El-'Amarneh*. London: Egypt Exploration Society.

Pendlebury, J.D.S. 1951. *City of Akhenaten*, III: *The Central City and Official Quarters*. London: Egypt Exploration Society.

Perepelkin, G. 1978. *The Secret of the Gold Coffin*. Moscow: Nauka Publishing House.

Pereyra De Fidanza, V. 2000. "A Queen Rewarding a Noblewoman in TT49." In *Les civilisations du bassin méditerranéen: Hommages à Joachim Sliwa*, edited by K.M. Ciałowicz and J.A. Ostrowski, 173–84. Cracow: Université Jagaellonne, Institut d'Archéologie.

Petrie, W.M.F. 1890. *Kahun, Gurob and Hawara*. London: Kegan Paul, Trench, Trübner, and Co.

———— 1892. *Medum*. London: D. Nutt.

———— 1894. *Tell el Amarna*. London: Methuen.

———— 1924. *A History of Egypt*. 7th ed. London: Methuen.

Philips, A.K. 1977. "Horemheb, Founder of the XIXth Dynasty? O. Cairo 25646 Reconsidered." *Orientalia* 46: 116–21.

Pierret, P. 1878. *Recueil d'Inscriptions inédites du Musée Égyptien du Louvre*. 2 vols. Paris: Librarie A. Franck.

Poláček, A. 1976. "Le décret d'Horemheb à Karnak: Essai d'analyse socio-juridique." In *Le Droit égyptien ancien: colloque organisé par l'Institut des Hautes Etudes de Belgique les 18 et 19 mars 1974 à l'initiative de Mr. Aristide Theodorides*, 87–111. Brussels: Institut des hautes études de Belgique.

Porter, B. and R.B. Moss. 1960–64; 1972; 1974–81; 1934; 1937; 1939; 1952. *Topographical Bibliography of Ancient Egyptian Hieroglyphic Texts, Reliefs and Paintings*, I: *The Theban Necropolis*, 2nd ed. by J. Málek; II: *Theban Temples*, 2nd edition by J. Málek; III: *Memphis*, 2nd ed. by J. Málek; IV: *Lower and Middle Egypt*; V: *Upper Egypt: Sites*; VI: *Upper Egypt: Chief Temples (excl. Thebes)*; VII, *Nubia, Deserts, and Outside Egypt*. Oxford: Clarendon Press/Griffith Institute.

Quibell, J.E. and A.G.K. Hayter. 1927. *Teti Pyramid, north side*. Cairo: Institut français d'Archéologie orientale.

Quiring, H. 1960. "Die Abkunft des Tutanchamon (1358–1351)." *Klio* 38: 53–61.

Ratié, S. 1986. "Quelques problèmes soulevés par la persécution de Toutankhamon." In *Hommages à François Daumas*, 545–50. Montpellier: Université de Montpellier.

Raven, M.J. 1994. "A sarcophagus for Queen Tiy and other fragments from the royal tomb at Amarna." *OMRO* 74: 7–20.

———— 2002. "The Tomb of Meryneith at Saqqara." *EgArch* 20: 26–28.

———— 2005. *The Tomb of Pay and Raia at Saqqara*. Leiden: National Museum of Antiquities/London: Egypt Exploration Society.

Raven, M.J., R. van Walsem, et al. (in preparation) *The Tomb of Meryneith at Saqqara*. Turnhout: Brepols.

Raven, M.J. 2001. *The Tomb of Maya and Meryt*, II: *Objects and Skeletal Remains*. Leiden: National Museum of Antiquities/London: Egypt Exploration Society.

———— (forthcoming) *The Memphite tomb of Horemheb, commander-in-chief of Tutankhamun*, V: *the forecourt and the area south of the tomb, with some notes on the tomb of Tia*. Turnhout: Brepols.

Redford, D.B. 1965. "The Coregency of Tuthmosis III and Amenophis II." *JEA* 51: 107–22.

———— 1966. "On the Chronology of the Egyptian Eighteenth Dynasty." *JNES* 25: 113–24.

———— 1967. *History and Chronology of the Eighteenth Dynasty of Egypt. Seven Studies*. Toronto: University of Toronto Press.

———— 1973a. "A New Dated Inscription from the Reign of Horemheb." *NSSEA* 4/1: 6–23.

———— 1973b. "New Light on the Asiatic Campaigning of Horemheb." *BASOR* 211: 36–49.

———— 1973c. "Studies on Akhenaten at Thebes, I: A report on the work of the Akhenaten Temple Project of the University Museum, University of Pennsylvania." *JARCE* 10: 77–94.

———— 1975. "Studies on Akhenaten at Thebes, II. A Report on the Work of the Akhenaten Temple Project of the University Museum, The University of Pennsylvania, for the Year 1973–4." *JARCE* 12: 9–18.

———— 1978–79. "Once Again the Filiation of Tutankhamun." *JSSEA* 9: 107–15.

———— 1984. *Akhenaten: The Heretic King*. Princeton: Princeton University Press.

———— 1988. *The Akhenaten Temple Project*, 2: Rwd-mnw, *Foreigners and Inscriptions*. Toronto: The Akhenaten Temple Project.

Reeves, C.N. 1978. "A Further Occurrence of Nefertiti as ḥmt nsw ꜥꜣt." *GM* 30: 61–69.

——— 1981. "A State Chariot from the Tomb of Ay?" *GM* 46: 11–19.

——— 1982. "Tuthmosis IV as 'great-grandfather' of Tutʿankhamūn." *GM* 56: 65–69.

——— 1988. "New Light on Kiya from Texts in the British Museum." *JEA* 74: 91–101.

——— 1990a. *Valley of the Kings: The decline of a royal necropolis.* London & New York: Kegan Paul International.

——— 1990b. *The Complete Tutankhamun: The King, the Tomb, the Royal Treasure.* London: Thames & Hudson.

——— 2001. *Akhenaten: Egypt's False Prophet.* London: Thames & Hudson.

Robichon, C. and A. Varille. 1936. *Le Temple du scribe royal Amenhotep, fils de Hapou.* Cairo: Institut français d'Archéologie orientale.

——— 1938. "Fouilles des temples funéraires Thébains (1937)." *RdE* 3: 99–102.

Robins, G. 1981. "ḥmt nsw wrt Meritaton." *GM* 52: 75–81.

——— 1984. "Two Statues from the Tomb of Tutankhamun." *GM* 71: 47–50.

——— 1987. "The role of the royal family in the 18th dynasty up to the reign of Amenhotpe III: 2. Royal children." *Wepwawet* 3: 15–17.

——— 1991. "The Mother of Tutankhamun." *DE* 20: 71–73.

——— 1992. "The Mother of Tutankhamun (2)." *DE* 22: 25–27.

——— 1994. *Proportion and Style in Ancient Egyptian Art.* London: Thames & Hudson.

Roeder, G. 1924. *Ägyptische Inschriften aus den Staatlichen Museen zu Berlin.* 2 vols. Leipzig: J.C. Hinrichs.

——— 1958. "Thronfolger und König Smench-ka-Rê (Dynastie XVIII)." *ZÄS* 83: 43–74.

——— 1969. *Amarna-Reliefs aus Hermopolis: Ausgrabungen der Deutschen Hermopolis-Expedition in Hermopolis 1929–1939.* Hildesheim: Verlag Gebrüder Gerstenberg.

Romer, J. 1975. "The Tomb of Tuthmosis III." *MDAIK* 31: 315–51.

——— 1981. *Valley of the Kings.* London: Michael Joseph.

Ryholt, K.S.B. 1997. *The Political Situation in Egypt During the Second Intermediate Period, c. 1800–1550 B.C.* Copenhagen: Museum Tusculanum Press.

Saʿad, R. 1975. "Fragments d'un monument de Toutânkamon retrouvés dans le IXᵉ pylône de Karnak." In *Cahiers de Karnak V: 1970–1972*, edited by J. Lauffray, S. Sauneron and R. Saʿad, 93–109. Cairo: Centre franco-égyptien d'Étude des Temples de Karnak.

Sadowska, M. 2000. "Semenchkare and Zannanza." *GM* 175: 73–77.

Samson, J. 1973. "Royal Inscriptions from Amarna." *CdE* 48: 243–50.

———— 1976. "Royal names in Amarna History." *CdE* 51: 30–38.

———— 1977. "Nefertiti's Regality." *JEA* 63: 88–97.

———— 1978. *Amarna, City of Akhenaton and Nefertiti: Nefertiti as Pharaoh.* Warminster: Aris & Phillips.

———— 1979. "Akhenaten's Successor." *GM* 32: 53–58.

———— 1982a. "Akhenaten's Coregent Ankhkheprure-Nefernefruaten." *GM* 53: 51–54.

———— 1982b. "Akhenaten's Coregent and Successor." *GM* 57: 57–59.

———— 1982c. "Nefernefruaten-Nefertiti 'Beloved of Akhenaten,' Ankhkheperure Nefernefruaten 'Beloved of Akhenaten,' Ankhkheprure Smenkhkare 'Beloved of the Aten.'" *GM* 57: 61–67.

———— 1982d. "The History of the Mystery of Akhenaten's Successor." In *L'Egyptologie en 1979, Axes prioritaires de recherches.* vol. 2, 291–97. Paris: Centre National de la Recherche Scientifique.

———— 1985. *Nefertiti and Cleopatra: Queen-Monarchs of Ancient Egypt.* London: Rubicon Press.

Sauneron, S. 1951. "La tradition officielle relative à la XVIIIe dynastie d'après un ostracon de la Vallée des Rois." *CdE* XXVI/51: 46–49.

Schaden, O. 1977. *The God's Father Ay.* PhD thesis, University of Minnesota. Ann Arbor: UMI.

———— 1979. "Preliminary Report on the Re-clearance of Tomb 25 in the Western Valley of the Kings (WV 25). University of Minnesota Egyptian Expedition January 1976." *ASAE* 63: 161–68.

———— 1984. "Clearance of the Tomb of King Ay (WV 23)." *JARCE* 21: 39–65.

———— 1992. "Courtier, Confidante, Counselor, King: The God's Father Ay." *Amarna Letters* 2: 92–114.

———— 2000. "Paintings in the Tomb of King Ay & the Western Valley of the Kings Project." *Amarna Letters* 4: 88–111.

Schäfer, H. 1918. "Altes und Neues zur Kunst und Religion von Tell el-Amarna." *ZÄS* 55: 1–43.

Schiaparelli, E. 1924. *Esplorazione della ››Valle delle Regine‹‹ nella necropoli di Tebe.* Turin: R. Museo di Antichità.

Schiff Giorgini, M. 1965, 1998–2003. *Soleb,* I, III–V. Florence: Sansoni/Cairo: Institut français d'Archéologie orientale.

Schmidt, H.C. 1994. "Ein Fall von Amtsanmassung? Die Gottesgemahlin Nefertari-Meritenmut." *GM* 140: 81–92.

Schneider, H.D. 1996. *The Memphite Tomb of Ḥoremḥeb, Commander-in-Chief of Tut'ankhamūn*, II: *Catalogue of the Finds*. Leiden: National Museum of Antiquities/London: Egypt Exploration Society.

Schulman, A.R. 1964a. "Some Observations on the Military Background of the Amarna Period." *JARCE* 3: 51–69.

——— 1964b. *Military Rank, Title and Organization in the Egyptian New Kingdom*. Berlin: Verlag Bruno Hessling.

——— 1964c. "Excursus on the 'Military Officer' Nakhtmin." *JARCE* 3: 124–26.

——— 1965. "The Berlin 'Trauerrelief' (No. 12411) and Some Officials of Tut'ankhamūn and Ay." *JARCE* 4: 55–68.

——— 1978. "Ankhesenamun, Nofretity, and the Amka Affair." *JARCE* 15: 43–48.

——— 1982. "The Nubian War of Akhenaten." In *L'Égyptologie en 1979, Axes prioritaires de recherches*, vol. 2, 299–16. Paris: Centre National de la Recherche Scientifique.

Seele, K.C. 1955. "King Ay and the Close of the Amarna Age." *JNES* 14: 168–80.

Sethe, K. 1905. "Die Schwägerin Amenophis' IV." *ZÄS* 42: 134–35.

Shannon, E. 1987. "Ring Bezels with Royal Names at the Workmen's Village 1979–1986." In *Amarna Reports*, edited by B.J. Kemp, IV, 154–59. London: Egypt Exploration Society.

Shaw, I. 1984. "Ring Bezels at Amarna." In *Amarna Reports*, edited by B.J. Kemp, I, 124–32. London: Egypt Exploration Society.

Simpson, W.K. 1963. *Heka-Nefer and the Dynastic Material from Toshka and Arminna*. New Haven: The Peabody Museum of Natural History of Yale University/Philadelphia: The University Museum of the University of Pennsylvania.

Smith, H.S. 1976. *The Fortress of Buhen*, II: *the Inscriptions*. London: Egypt Exploration Society.

Smith, R.W. and D.B. Redford. 1976. *The Akhenaten Temple Project*, 1: *Initial Discoveries*. Warminster: Aris & Phillips.

Spalinger, A.J. 1979. "Egyptian-Hittite Relations at the Close of the Amarna Period and Some Notes on Hittite Military Strategy in North Syria." *BES* 1: 55–89.

——— 1982. *Aspects of the Military Documents of the Ancient Egyptians*. New Haven: Yale University Press.

——— 2005. *War in Ancient Egypt*. Oxford: Blackwell.

Spencer, A.J. 1989. *Excavations at el-Ashmunein*, II: *The Temple Area*. London: British Museum Publications.

Stempel, R. 2007. "Identification of Nibhururiya and the synchronism in the Egyptian and Hittite chronology in light of a newly reconstructed Hittite text." *GM* 213: 97–100.

Stewart, H.M. 1976. *Egyptian Stelae, Reliefs and Paintings from the Petrie Collection*, I: *The New Kingdom*. Warminster: Aris & Phillips.

Strouhal, E. 2008. *The Memphite Tomb of Horemheb, Commander-in-Chief of Tutankhamun*, IV: *Skeletal Material*. London: Egypt Exploration Society.

Strouhal, E. and G. Callender. 1992. "A Profile of Queen Mutnodjmet." *BACE* 3: 67–75.

Strudwick, N. 1985. *The Administration of Egypt in the Old Kingdom: the Highest Titles and their Holders*. London: Kegan Paul International.

Tallet, P. 1996. "Une jarre de l'an 31 et une jarre de l'an 10 dans la cave de Toutânkhamon." *BIFAO* 96: 369–83.

Tawfik, S. 1975. "Aton Studies: 3. Back again to Nefer-nefru-Aton." *MDAIK* 31: 159–68.

———— 1981. "Aton Studies: 6. Was Nefernefruaten the Immediate Successor of Akhenaten?" *MDAIK* 37: 469–73.

———— 1991. "Recently Excavated Ramesside Tombs at Saqqara: 1. Architecture." *MDAIK* 47: 403–409.

———— 1994. "Tutanchamuns Grab. Provisorium oder kunstvolles Novum?" In *Quaerentes scientiam : Festgabe für Wolfhart Westendorf zu seinem 70. Geburtstag überreicht von seinen Schülern*, edited by H. Behlmer. Göttingen: Seminar für Ägyptologie und Koptologie.

Tawfik, T.S. 2003. "The Extent of the New Kingdom Cemetery in the Memphite Necropolis." In *Egyptology at the Dawn of the Twenty-First Century: Proceedings of the Eighth International Congress of Egyptologists, Cairo, 2000*, edited by Z. Hawass and L.P. Brock. vol. 1, 508–13. Cairo: The American University in Cairo Press.

Thiem, A.-C. 2000. *Speos von Gebel es-Silsileh. Analyse der architektonischen und ikonographischen Konzeption im Rahmen des politischen und legitimatorischen Programmes der Nachamarnazeit*. 2 vols. Wiesbaden: Harrassowitz.

Thomas, E. 1967. "Was Queen Mutnedjemet the Owner of Tomb 33 in the Valley of the Queens?" *JEA* 53: 161–63.

Traunecker, C. and Traunecker, F. 1984–85. "Sur la-salle dite 'du couronnement' à Tell-el-Amarna." *BSEG* 9–10: 285–307.

Troy, L. 1986. *Patterns of Queenship in Ancient Egyptian Myth and History*. Uppsala: Boreas.

van Dijk, J. 1988. "The Development of the Memphite Necropolis in the Post-Amarna Period." In *Memphis et ses nécropoles au Nouvel Empire: Nouvelles données, nouvelles questions*, edited by A.-P. Zivie, 37–46. Paris: Editions du CNRS.

—— 1990. "The Overseer of the Treasury Maya: a biographical sketch." *OMRO* 70: 23–28.

—— 1993. *The New Kingdom Necropolis of Memphis. Historical and Iconographical Studies.* Groningen: Proefschrift Rijksuniversiteit Groningen.

—— 1995. "Maya's Chief Sculptor Userhat-Hatiay. With a Note on the Length of the Reign of Horemheb." *GM* 148: 29–34.

—— 1996. "Horemheb and the Struggle for the Throne of Tutankhamun." *BACE* 7: 29–42.

—— 1997. "The Noble Lady of Mitanni and Other Royal Favourites of the Eighteenth Dynasty." In *Essays on Ancient Egypt in Honour of Hermann te Velde*, edited by J. van Dijk, 33–46. Groningen: Styx Publications.

—— 2006. "The Death of Meketaten." In *Causing His Name to Live: Studies in Egyptian Epigraphy and History in Memory of William J. Murnane*, edited by P. Brand. <http://history.memphis.edu/murnane/>.

—— 2008. "New evidence on the length of reign of Horemheb." In *Tenth International Congress of Egyptologists: Abstracts of Papers*, edited by P. Kousoulis, 253–54. Rhodes: University of the Aegean, Department of Mediterranean Studies.

van Dijk, J. and M. Eaton-Krauss. 1986. "Tutankhamun at Memphis." *MDAIK* 42: 35–41.

van Dijk, J., et al. (in preparation). *The Tomb of Maya and Meryt*, I: *Architecture and Reliefs*.

Van Siclen, C.C. 2005a. "Soundings South of the Eighth Pylon at Karnak." *ASAE* 79: 187–89.

—— 2005b. "La cour du IXe pylône à Karnak." *BSFE* 163: 27–46.

Vandersleyen, C. 1984–85. "L'iconographie de Toutankhamon et les effigies provenant de sa tombe." *BSEG* 9–10: 309–21.

—— 1992. "Royal figures from Tut'ankhamūn's tomb: their historical usefulness." In *After Tut'ankhamūn*, edited by C.N. Reeves, 73–84. London and New York: Kegan Paul International.

Vandier, J. 1968. "La statue d'un grand prêtre de Mendès." *JEA* 54: 89–94.

Vergnieux, R. and M. Gondran. 1997. *Aménophis IV et les pierres du soleil. Akhénaton retrouvé.* Paris: Arthaud.

Vergote, J. 1961. *Toutankhamon dans les archives Hittites*. Istanbul: Nederlands Historisch-Archaeologisch Instituut in het Nabije Oosten.

von Beckerath, J. 1995. "Das Problem der Regierungsdauer Haremhabs." *SAK* 22: 37–41.

———— 1997. *Chronologie des Pharaonischen Ägypten*. Mainz: Philipp von Zabern.

———— 1999. *Handbuch der ägyptischen Königsnamen*. 2nd ed. Mainz: Phillip von Zabern.

Waddell, W.G. (trans.) 1940. *Manetho*. Cambridge, MA: Harvard University Press/London: William Heinemann.

Weatherhead, F. 2007. *Amarna Palace Paintings*. London: Egypt Exploration Society.

Weeks, K.R. 2000. *KV5: A Preliminary Report*. Cairo: The American University in Cairo Press.

Wegner, J. 1996. "The Nature and Chronology of the Senwosret III-Amenemhat III Regnal Succession: Some Considerations Based on New Evidence from the Mortuary Temple of Senwosret III at Abydos." *JNES* 55: 249–79.

Weigall, A. 1910. *The Life and Times of Akhnaton*. Edinburgh: William Blackwood and Sons.

———— 1924. *Ancient Egyptian Works of Art*. London: T.F. Unwin.

Wildung, D. 1977. "Hoherpriester von Memphis." *LÄ* II: 1256–1263.

———— 1998. "Le frère aîné d'Ekhnaton: réflexions sur un décès prématuré." *BSFE* 143: 10–18.

Wilkinson, T.A.H. 2000. *The Royal Annals of Ancient Egypt: the Palermo Stone and its associated fragments*. London and New York: Kegan Paul International.

Yoshimura, S. and J. Kondo. 1995. "Excavations at the tomb of Amenophis III." *EgArch* 17–18.

Yoyotte, J. 1982–83. "Le dieu Horemheb." *RdE* 34: 148–49.

Zivie, A.-P. 1990. *Decouverte à Saqqarah: le vizir oublié*. Paris: Seuil.

———— 1998. "The tomb of the lady Maïa, wet-nurse of Tutankhamun." *EgArch* 13: 7–8.

———— 2000. "La résurrection des hypogées du Nouvel Empire à Saqqara." In *Abusir and Saqqara in the Year 2000*, edited by M. Barta and J. Krejčí, 173–92. Prague: Academy of Sciences of the Czech Republic.

———— 2007. *The Lost Tombs of Saqqara*. Np: cara.cara edition/Cairo: The American University in Cairo Press.

Zivie, C.M. 1976. *Giza au deuxième millénaire*. Cairo: Institut français d'Archéologie orientale.

INDEX

For the use of number and letters to distinguish homonyms, see Dodson and Hilton 2004. Reigning monarchs of Egypt are capitalized; illustrations shown in **bold**.

Mnevis bull 74
Montju 63, 124
Montjuhotep A (father of Sobhotep III) 96
Montjuhotep I (God's Father) 96
MONTJUHOTEP II **133**, 134
Mose (Scribe of the Treasury of Ptah) 129–30, 160 n.124
Munich, Staatliche Sammlung Ägyptische Kunst, object Gl.93 **4**
Murshilish II (King of Hatti) 53, 92, 166–69
Mushilish III (Urhi-Teshub, King of Hatti) 168–69
Mut 46–47, 48, **49**, 50, 63, 68, **70**, **78**, **81**, clergy of 101
Mutbenret 98; *see also* Mutnodjmet
Mutemnub (mother of Ay B) 101
Mutemwia (mother of Amenhotep III) 157 n.115
Mutnodjmet (sister of Nefertiti) 47, 98–99, 146 n.89
Mutnodjmet (wife of Horemheb) 98–99, 103, 114–18, **119**, 155 n.50, 157 nn.18, 33, 160 n.129
Muwatallish II (King of the Hittites) 168–69

Nag el-Hammam 126
Nakhtmin A (Judge) 101
Nakhtmin B (Generalissimo) **81**, 83, **98**, 99, 101–102, 112, 114, 150 n.78, 154 n.31
Nakhtmin C (high priest of Min) **102**, 104, 107
Nakhtmin Q (Overseer of Works at Akhmim) 103
Napkhuriya (Akkadian form of Neferkheperure) 55
National Museum of Scotland *see* Edinburgh, National Museum of Scotland
Nay (God's Father) 102
Nazibugash (King of Babylon) 166–67
Nazimaruttash (King of Babylon) 166–69

Nebkheperure *see* Tutankhamun; Tutankhaten
Nebmaatre (high priest at Heliopolis) 139 n.13
Neferkheperure *see* Akhenaten
NEFERHOTEP I 96
Neferhotep i (Chief Scribe of Amun: TT49) 102
Neferhotep ii (God's Father of Amun-Re: TT50) 126, 161 n.139
Neferkheperuhirsekheper (TA13) **28**
NEFERNEFERUATEN **33**, 34–40, **34**, **35**, 42–47, **43**, **44**, **45**, 49–52, 55–56, 61, 78, 83, 88, 108, 112, 116, 128, 138, 144 nn.29, 41, 147 n.118, 160 n.124, 163; 166–67
Neferneferuaten-Nefertiti *see* Nefertiti
Neferneferuaten-tasherit (daughter of Akhenaten) 13, **14**, 18, **20–21**, 23, 37, 145 n.46
Neferneferure (daughter of Akhenaten) 13, **14**, 23, 142 n.53
Neferrenpet (vizier) 151 n.102
Nefertiry D (wife of Rameses II) 108, 118, 157 n.33
Nefertiti **8–9**, 13, 15–18, **22**, 24–25, **25**, 29, 35–40, **37**, 42–44, **44**, 47, **48**, 66, 68, 89, 97–99, 107, 114, 116, 138, 140 n.9, 142 nn.37, 42, 143 n.68; *see also* Neferneferuaten
New York, Metropolitan Museum of Art, objects: 23.10.1 **66**; 45.4.7 153 n.4, 154 n.15
Nipkhururiya (Akkadian form of Nebkheperure) 60, 89, 91
Nukhashshe (north Syrian polity) 54, 56

Opet Festival 71, 112
Osiris **124**

Paatenemheb (General: TA24) 109
Pahemnetjer (Egyptian Resident in north Syria) 54